"If you want to understand the times, culture, message, and life of Daniel, James R. Coggins's *Living for God in a Pagan Society: What Daniel Can Teach Us* is a must read. It is accessible (easy to read), informative (filled with history and explanatory notes) and applicable to our time. Looking at the early chapters of the book of Daniel, Coggins leads us into that world with an eye on how we, the people of God, can live in today's pagan-bent world. This vital and important treatment of this critical moment in the ancient world will be helpful for study groups, pastoral preaching and personal reflection on the ways of God, then and today."

– Brian C. Stiller, Global Ambassador
The World Evangelical Alliance

"In his relatively concise look at the book of Daniel, James R. Coggins gives helpful insights into the background, meaning and application of this Old Testament prophet. While one will not find a detailed interpretation of the 'prophetic' elements of the book (this is not Coggins's intent), this volume does provide the reader with a glimpse of the stories that run parallel to the prophecies and stimulates reflection on their meaning for life in the 21st century. Coggins does a good job of helping us understand the narratives and what we can learn from them. Recommended as an aid for Bible teachers and preachers who want to get some practical handles on an ancient text."

– Ron Redekop, Senior Pastor
Richmond Alliance Church, Richmond, BC

Living for God
in a
Pagan Society

What Daniel Can Teach Us

By
James R. Coggins

Mill Lake Books

Copyright © 2019 by James R. Coggins
No part of this book may be reproduced in any form without written permission, except for brief quotations in critical reviews.

Published by Mill Lake Books
Abbotsford, BC
Canada

Printed by Lightning Source, distributed by Ingram

Unless otherwise noted, Scripture verses are taken from THE HOLY BIBLE, NEW INTERNATIONAL VERSION®, NIV® Copyright © 1973, 1978, 1984, 2011 by Biblica, Inc.® Used by permission. All rights reserved worldwide.

Scripture verses designated NASB are taken from the New American Standard Bible Copyright © 1960, 1962, 1963, 1968, 1971, 1972, 1973, 1975, 1977, 1995 by The Lockman Foundation.

ISBN: 978-0-9951983-8-8

Table of Contents

Introduction: A Pagan Society?..7
Chapter 1: A Pagan Society (Daniel 1:1-7)..9
    The City of God and the City of Babylon
    Defeat
    False Hope
Chapter 2: Moral Man in Immoral Society (Daniel 1:8-21)............17
    Eat Your Vegetables
    Everyone's Doing It
    No Excuses
    Facing the Pressure
Chapter 3: Now is the Time to Worship (Daniel 2).........................25
    What's It All About?
    Pagan Religion
    Responding to a Crisis
    The God Who Answers
    The Vision
    The Purpose and Meaning of the Dream
    It's Our Turn
Chapter 4: Now is the Time to Worship, Part 2 (Daniel 3)............39
    He Just Doesn't Get It
    The Wise Men
    Hananiah, Mishael and Azariah
    Nations and Peoples of Every Language
    Modern Questions
Chapter 5: You Can Make a Difference (Daniel 4)............................51
    A Question to Ponder
    The Form
    The Same Old Story
    The Message of God
    God's Purpose
    The Fulfillment of God's Purpose
    Collateral Conversions
    The Wise Men
    The God of History
    Dare to Be a Daniel

Chapter 6: Love Your Enemies (Jeremiah 29:1-23) 73
    The Context
    The Content
    The Promise
    How Do We Know Which Prophets Are Right Today?
    The Commands

Chapter 7: Hanging in over the Long Haul (Daniel 5) 97
    The New King
    The Message
    The Issues
    Daniel's End

Chapter 8: Standing in the Need of Prayer (Daniel 6) 109
    The Setting
    Office Politics
    Blinded by Power
    Daniel
    The Outcome
    The Point of It All
    Bringing It Home

Chapter 9:
Where Can We Go to Learn about God? (Daniel 9:1-23) 125
    The Context
    Understanding from the Scriptures
    Answered Prayer
    Bringing It Home

Chapter 10: Doing Exploits (Daniel 7-12) 137
    First Vision (Daniel 7)
    Second Vision (Daniel 8)
    Third Vision (Daniel 9)
    Fourth Vision (Daniel 10-12)
    Who Is in Control?
    The People Who Know Their God

Study Guide 151
My Commitment 161

Introduction
A Pagan Society?

Do you ever feel confused or disappointed with what is going on in the world? Do you feel helpless before unwelcome trends in society that are beyond your control? Are you unsure of what you should do about it?

This is evidence that we are living in a pagan, God-defying society. Don't believe it? Don't want to believe it? The vast majority of North American cultural endeavors (movies, television, music and books) seem dedicated to the spread of violence, sexual immorality and selfishness. Evolution, atheism and moral relativism dominate intellectual discussion in our universities. In a survey, three-quarters of North Americans said they would cheat, steal and lie if it would be to their advantage. Sexual promiscuity is now considered the norm, and half of North American marriages end in divorce, even among evangelical Christians.

In Canada, where I live, it is generally a political advantage to be a practicing homosexual, and evangelical Christians are ridiculed as foolish or hateful—or both. Over half a century ago, between sixty and seventy percent of Canadians attended church every week; today only about twenty percent of Canadians do. Christians are slowly being squeezed out of government, the media, universities, and the teaching, medical and legal professions.

In the United States, the situation does not seem nearly as bad, but the same trends are in place. Church attendance has now dropped below forty percent and is continuing to drop.

If this analysis is right—and even if it is only partly right, it is clear that we face strong pressure from pagan, God-defying forces within our society—then what? Is the triumph of evil inevitable? Are we doomed to watch helplessly while the world collapses around us? What, if anything, can we do? How can we live for God in a God-defying society?

This book invites you to put yourself in Daniel's place.

You may remember the story of Daniel and the lions' den from Sunday school in your childhood. But Daniel's problems started long before he was thrown into the lions' den. Daniel was at risk of being thrown into the lions' den because he was a member of the people of God who had been carried off into exile in a pagan society.

If you are a Christian living in North America, you *are* in Daniel's place. You, a believer in the true God, are living in a pagan culture. This is why Daniel's story is relevant to you.

Chapter 1
A Pagan Society
Daniel 1:1-7

The City of God and the City of Babylon

Jerusalem, the capital city of the people of God, was an impressive city with strong fortifications, magnificent palaces and a beautiful temple. Under King David and King Solomon a thousand years before Christ, it had been the capital of a great empire. At the crossroads of Asia, Europe and Africa, it had dominated the world. But, by Daniel's time, the truth is that Jerusalem was an old and faded city. Its foundations were crumbling, and its defenders were few. The temple of God in Jerusalem had been a beautiful structure, lined with gold, when it had been built 400 years earlier, but it had been looted several times since, sometimes by enemies and sometimes by Jewish kings who had used the gold to buy off enemies or to worship other gods. It also was old and decaying.

In contrast, the city of Babylon, to which Daniel was carried into exile, was a far more impressive city. Jerusalem covered less than a square mile. Babylon was twenty to twenty-five times that size. It was protected by a massive double wall so wide that two chariots could travel on top of it side by side. Ancient accounts say the wall was 300 feet high, was 25 feet thick and extended 35 feet below ground. Inside that wall was another massive defensive wall. Entry through Babylon's northern gate led to the great 1000-yard-long "Processional Way," bounded on both sides by massive walls decorated with larger-than-life carvings of 120 lions, symbols of the Babylonian goddess Ishtar, and 570 dragons and bulls, symbols of the Babylonian gods Marduk and Bel. While Jerusalem had an impressive temple, Babylon had at least fifty-three, some of them larger than the temple in Jerusalem and many of them filled with massive gold idols. There were at least two royal palaces in the city. Attached to one were the hanging gardens, one of the "seven wonders of the ancient world," built upon a series of massive arches and columns to resemble the lush mountain homeland of Babylon's foreign queen. The city was built in a fertile valley, watered by the Euphrates and Tigris Rivers and a series of carefully engineered canals.

Babylon was the capital city of the Babylonian Empire, a fabulously wealthy and powerful empire that stretched from India to Egypt. In comparison, the nation of Judah was small and powerless, the last remaining tribe of what had once been the twelve tribes of Israel, an outpost on the way to the riches of Egypt. What happened when Judah and Babylon collided is scarcely surprising: What happened when the Babylonian Empire and the people of God collided was that the people of God were soundly defeated.

Defeat

Militarily, the Jewish army was no match for the Babylonian army. King Solomon had had 1200 chariots and 14,000 horses (1 Kings 10:26) and an army of hundreds of thousands. Four centuries later, the entire Jewish army numbered only 7,000 men (2 Kings 24:16). The Babylonian army, in contrast, probably numbered in the hundreds of thousands. In 605 BC, the Babylonian army overran the Egyptian army at Carchemish, far to the north of Judah near what is now the border between Syria and Turkey. The Babylonian army then marched south, passing virtually unopposed through the country of Judah, taking anything of value and shipping it back to Babylon. Also sent off to Babylon were the best and brightest among those who would have become Judah's next generation of leaders, including Daniel and his friends. Politically, Judah, which had been subordinate to Egypt, became subordinate to Babylon, owing loyalty to the Babylonian Empire and paying annual tribute (taxes) to Babylon.

Religiously, in those days, the power of a god was thought to be linked to the power of the nation state which worshiped that god. Thus, the Babylonian gods were thought to have proven themselves more powerful than Judah's God, Yahweh (translated as upper-case "LORD" in most English Bibles). As a symbol of this, gold articles were taken from the temple of Yahweh in Jerusalem and placed in the temples of the Babylonian gods in Babylon. As Judah paid tribute to Babylon and recognized its superior power, so this action symbolized that Yahweh was paying tribute to the Babylonian gods, recognizing their superior power. But the situation was even worse than that. In fact, the name Yahweh does not even occur in the Book of Daniel until the ninth chapter. Even most of "the people of God" in Jerusalem had long since ceased to worship Yahweh, the true God, and were worshiping "gods" just like their pagan neighbors.

Culturally and intellectually, Babylonian fashions, styles and ideas influenced the nations Babylon had conquered. Daniel and his three friends, for instance, were to be trained in the language and literature of the Babylonians. Babylon very carefully controlled the educational system. The Babylonians took the elite people from the nations they conquered and indoctrinated them to think like Babylonians. The book of Daniel is unique among the books of the Old Testament part of the Bible. Except for parts of the book of Ezra and a few isolated verses in other books, the rest of the Old Testament is written in Hebrew, the language of the Israelites. Much of Daniel (2:4-7:28) is written in Aramaic, the diplomatic language of the Babylonian Empire. The Babylonians even tried to force Daniel and his friends to eat Babylonian food the way the Babylonians ate it.

Economically, Babylon controlled trade and commerce and was fabulously wealthy. It was known as "a land of merchants" (Ezekiel 16:29). Revelation, the last book of the Bible, speaks of a mysterious "mark of the beast"; either the Roman Empire or some future evil anti-Christian empire (or both) would require people to accept this mark on their hands or foreheads as a sign of loyalty before they would be allowed to buy and sell (Revelation 13:16-17; 14:9-11; 16:2; 19:20; 20:4). The idea is not new. Economics has long been used as a means of control. The powerful dominate trade, forbid their enemies to trade (via tariffs, boycotts, embargoes and blockades) and make sure that any trade that is carried on will primarily benefit them. Six hundred years before Christ, the Babylonian Empire controlled world trade.

Babylonian control extended even to individuals. Even today, if we were to ask who Hananiah, Mishael and Azariah were, even most Christians would have no idea. They are Daniel's three friends, yet today we know them not by their original Hebrew names but by the names the Babylonians gave them, Shadrach, Meshach and Abednego. This is no small thing because names are tied to identity and when you change someone's name, you change that person's identity. Hananiah (which means in Hebrew "Yahweh has been gracious") was renamed Shadrach. Mishael ("Who is as God?") was renamed Meshach ("Who is this?")—perhaps a deliberate insult to Mishael or to Yahweh, suggesting that neither Mishael nor Mishael's God had any real identity of their own, but only what the Babylonians gave them. Azariah ("Yahweh has helped") was renamed Abednego ("servant of the god Nebo"). Daniel ("God is my judge") also was renamed after a pagan god; his new name was Belteshazzar ("Bel, protect the king"). Daniel and his friends were not allowed to choose their own careers or place of residence. They were taken away from their homes into exile and conscripted into the civil service of the Babylonian Empire, becoming part of the structure which oppressed their own people. They were most likely castrated, so that they would have no families and would have no loyalties other than to serve Babylon. They remained in this position for the rest of their lives; there was no escape.

False Hope

What does this sad history have to do with us? If we are Christians living in North America, the fact is that we also have been defeated by powerful pagan forces which now dominate our society. When I wrote the first draft of this book and suggested the title *Living for God in a Pagan Society*, my agent protested, "The book will never sell in the US. American Christians are convinced that theirs is a Christian nation. They won't believe that they are living in a pagan society." Yet the fact remains that, by and large, we have lost the battle for the hearts and minds of North Americans, and the government, the media, the education system and the economic system have been taken over by others.

This may not be obvious to us, but it was not obvious to the Jews in Daniel's time either. When Nebuchadnezzar took possession of Judah, he did not destroy it. Instead, he left the Jewish King Jehoiakim on the throne and demanded that the Jews pay annual tribute (money and goods, taxes) to Babylon. He did not want to destroy the people of God so much as to make the people of God his servants.

This situation fooled the Jews for a long time. In 597, eight years after Daniel and his friends went into exile, the next Jewish king, Jehoiachin, rebelled against Babylon. The Babylonian army simply marched in again, replaced Jehoiachin with his uncle, Mattaniah (renamed Zedekiah), and took more people and goods to Babylon. But Jerusalem was still standing, Yahweh was still being worshiped in the temple, and a Jewish king was on the throne. Moreover, many of the Jews saw Babylonian domination as only a temporary aberration. Indeed, some of their prophets told the Jews that God would soon deliver the Jews from the Babylonians as He had delivered them from previous enemies and that the people of God would soon be able to drive the pagan invaders from the Promised Land once again. (See the false prophecy of Hananiah—a different man than Daniel's friend—in Jeremiah 28.)

But this was all an illusion. The war had been lost. Pagan Babylon was firmly in control. The situation endured for almost twenty years, from 605 BC, when Daniel and his friends were taken into exile, to 587 BC. About 589 BC King Zedekiah, believing the optimistic predictions of his prophets, refused to pay any more tribute and rebelled against Babylon. But the people of God were weak. In many ways, they were as pagan, immoral and faithless as the Babylonians and the other pagan peoples around them. The rebellion was hopeless. Babylon's response was predictable. Nebuchadnezzar sent his army. This time, Jerusalem was overrun after a brutal two-year siege, Yahweh's temple was destroyed, Jerusalem's fortifications were leveled, the city was burned, many Jews were slaughtered, and most of the rest were shipped off into exile. (The whole sad history is told in 2 Kings 24-25, 2 Chronicles 36 and Jeremiah 39.)

So it is with us. Many North American Christians still have the illusion of influence and power and godliness. We still have national prayer breakfasts and national slogans that mention God. But these are largely empty symbols. The reality is much different. With the media, education, culture and the courts all dominated by pagans, a bleak and terrifying future seems inevitable.

Maybe our Jerusalem will not fall, but it is still true that we live in a society in which the power of pagans seems greater than the power of God's people. Hollywood can produce seductive movies for $100 million or $500 million or more, while Christians mostly have to make do with $1 million "films." If a major Christian movie is made, it is celebrated as a rare and gratifying event. Atheists dominate state universities with massive funding and tens of thousands of students while Christians struggle to maintain smaller, less adequately funded colleges. Billion-dollar radio and television networks bombard us with anti-Christian, self-centered and pleasure-seeking messages while smaller Christian stations struggle to stay on the air. It is easy to feel intimidated.

The question remains. Given the current situation, what can we do? Is it possible at all to resist the powers of evil? Can we really live for God in a God-defying society?

The remaining chapters in this book present some clear and practical things that we can do.

Chapter 2
Moral Man in Immoral Society
Daniel 1:8-21

Eat Your Vegetables

We are probably so familiar with this story that we don't realize how remarkable it is. Daniel, Hananiah, Mishael and Azariah refused to eat the royal "food" and "wine" and instead asked for "vegetables" and "water." The words for "food" and "wine" (*pathbag* and *yayin*) specifically refer to "meat" and fermented "wine" (*pathbag* is a Persian word). "Water" is the usual Hebrew word (*mayim*) for water, although it sometimes could be used figuratively for juice. The term "vegetables" refers to something planted (*zeroa*) and so would include bread, fruits and vegetables. The official replied in verse 10 that the king had determined their food (*maakal,* a more general word for "food"). So, the four young men essentially asked for a vegetarian diet.

What is the point of this story? That we should all be vegetarians? That we should eat a healthy diet? What was wrong with eating the king's meat and wine?

There were two things wrong with eating the king's meat and wine. First, in the Old Testament, God had given His people strict dietary laws to set them apart from other people. Food, especially meat, had to be prepared in certain specific ways (the blood had to be drained, for instance, and the internal organs and fat were not to be eaten). Since

Nebuchadnezzar's meat was not prepared according to Jewish laws, it would have been a sin for the four young men to eat it. Second, the king's meat and wine would have been consecrated to the Babylonian gods in the Babylonian temples. If the Jewish boys ate it, they would be in essence worshiping the Babylonian gods, uniting with them by eating their food. This would have been idolatrous, and it would thus have been sinful for the Jewish boys to eat and drink the king's food.

So the boys convinced one of the king's officials to let them try eating vegetables and water for ten days. It turned out that this diet was healthier than the diet everyone else was eating. This again does not necessarily mean that a vegetarian diet is healthier and we should all become vegetarians. In one sense, the boys' health was a blessing of God for their obedience. In another sense, it is true that the king's diet was unhealthy. Meat in most societies is more expensive than vegetables, and so there is a temptation for the rich to display their wealth by eating a lot of meat, too much meat. Moreover, kings liked to eat fat meat. Such a diet would be unbalanced and unhealthy. Once in our life, my wife and I went on a cruise (for our 25th wedding anniversary). The food was wonderful, huge helpings of rich desserts and rich meats—but a week was long enough. If we had eaten like that every day of our lives, we would have died young. We know that the meat-rich North American diet leads to obesity and cancer. Similarly, beverages with a high alcohol content are not healthy. Yet the healthy results for Daniel and his three friends were only a byproduct. For God and the four young Jews, the more important issue was the moral one, obeying and worshiping only the true God.

Everyone's Doing It

Now, we need to put the issue into perspective, put the issue into the larger context of Daniel and his three friends. The Babylonians had overwhelmed the people of God. Jerusalem and God's temple were in danger of being destroyed. Daniel and his friends were enduring exile and had been castrated. They were being tempted to worship idols and in danger of being indoctrinated by the Babylonian educational system. As captured members of a defeated race, they could be executed at any moment on the slimmest of pretexts. In such a situation, with so many other pressing problems, why were they worried about a minor issue like dietary regulations?

Daniel and his friends would have had a lot of excuses for not making an issue of the royal food. For one thing, they were slaves who had no control over their lives. They went where they were told to go. They did the jobs they were assigned to do. And if they didn't obey, they could be killed like so many of their compatriots would be in the coming years. Their lives had been spared on the condition that they serve the king of Babylon. In such a situation, surely God wouldn't care about a little food. Surely, when so many of God's people had been killed, their first duty was to preserve their lives. Surely they had to obey orders.

And what difference would it make anyway? If they refused the royal food, which would be an unforgivable insult to the king, they would be killed, or starved until they ate what they were told to eat. The Babylonians wouldn't notice or care. What good could come of refusing to eat the food?

As well, Daniel and his friends were young, probably young teenagers. They had not even finished their education. They were not experts in the Jewish law. Maybe they had misunderstood what the Bible really taught. They were barely out of childhood, accustomed to obeying adults. Would it really make sense for them to risk their lives over doctrines they weren't sure of?

Daniel and his friends were also alone, in exile in a foreign country, several months' journey from home (a longer journey away from home than anywhere on the earth today), and they had been taken away from their families. They had no support from their parents or religious leaders or teachers. If they went along with the Babylonian diet, their parents and teachers would most likely never know about it.

Further, if anyone could ever use the excuse "Everyone is doing it," it was Daniel and his friends. They weren't the only Jews taken into exile. They were "among" those taken to Babylon for training (Daniel 1:6). They were among dozens, perhaps hundreds of other young Jews of noble birth who had been taken to Babylon and conscripted into the Babylonian civil service. And not only were the Babylonians going along with Babylonian laws, but so were all these other Jews, some of them no doubt older than Daniel and his friends. But not one of them raised any objections to the Babylonian diet. If anyone could ever use the excuse "Everyone's doing it," it was these boys. And since Daniel is the only one who raised the issue, perhaps his three friends might have knuckled under too. Verse 11 suggests that the other three might have gotten involved only because they happened to be placed under the same guard as Daniel; they were essentially roommates.

No Excuses

There were a lot of excuses. The amazing thing is that Daniel doesn't seem to have even considered the excuses. He "resolved not to defile himself with the royal food and wine" (Daniel 1:8). When all the other exiles were quite naturally focused on ensuring their own survival, Daniel was focused on serving God. That was his priority. Jesus told His followers: "Do not worry, saying, 'What shall we eat?' or 'What shall we drink?' or 'What shall we wear?' For the pagans run after all these things, and your heavenly Father knows that you need them. But seek first his kingdom and his righteousness, and all these things will be given to you as well" (Matthew 6:31-33). That is what Daniel did, and in response God did what Jesus later promised—He took care of Daniel and his friends.

It is interesting as well that Daniel did not panic or mount a public protest or make demands. He quietly asked for permission. This respectfully recognized Babylonian civil authority while still insisting on God's overriding divine authority. He did not see the Babylonians as the enemy necessarily but recognized sin and evil as the real enemy of all human beings.

It is also instructive that Daniel was persistent in this matter. He asked the chief official for permission to change his diet. That official was favorable to Daniel—he liked the boy—but he refused permission because he was afraid of the king. At that point, Daniel might have said, "Oh, well. I tried," and then given up and accepted the king's diet. But when the chief official turned him down, he made the same appeal to the lower official in charge of Daniel and his three friends. And this time he was successful.

Obeying God's dietary laws might have seemed like a small thing, but it was a small thing that fell within Daniel's power and responsibility. He could not undo the Babylonian victory over his own people, the people of God. It did not appear that he could do anything about the idolatry and wickedness of the Babylonians—or even about the idolatry and wickedness of the Jews. But the one thing he could do something about was his own life. He could resolve that, whatever was going on around him, he personally would not defile himself with sin.

Facing the Pressure

What has this to do with us? The pressures we face are far less than those faced by Daniel and his friends. We in North America live in a society that promises human rights and freedom of religion. Many of us have support networks of godly parents and church leaders. Yet we still face similar pressures to disobey God's laws. The media, schools and our peers seem intent on leading us astray. Everyone seems to be doing it.

What can we do? Maybe we can't stop our society from peddling pornography, carrying out a million abortions a year or oppressing the poor. Maybe we can't help the fact that a majority of our fellow citizens say they would lie, cheat or steal "when necessary." Maybe we feel discouraged when we realize that sexual promiscuity now seems to be the accepted norm or that addictions of various kinds are wreaking havoc in our society. Maybe we can't change the fact that a majority of North Americans have premarital sex before marriage and extra-marital sex after marriage or that a majority of North American marriages will end in divorce. Maybe we feel helpless before the onslaught of violence and crime around us. But there is one thing we are responsible for and can control. We can say with Daniel, whatever happens in the society around us, "I will not defile myself."

We may think that a little sin doesn't matter, that compared to what everyone else is doing we're pretty good, that God can still use us in spite of some minor moral flaws and personality quirks. Hey, nobody's perfect, right? God does not see it that way. He says, "Be perfect, therefore, as your heavenly Father is perfect" (Matthew 5:48).

We may also ask: Does it really matter what one person does? Well, maybe we won't be completely alone or without influence. Daniel wasn't. He had his three friends. But does it really matter what even four people do? Maybe not. But the actions of Daniel and his friends, beginning with this one act of obedience, this one step of commitment, laid the groundwork for a series of events which profoundly rocked the foundations of the pagan society around them, and they are still having a profound effect on the world over 2,600 years later. What Daniel and his friends did in refusing to eat unholy food was a small thing. But if they had not been faithful in this small thing, it is unlikely that they would have been able to be faithful in any larger things, and it is unlikely that we would ever have heard about them. We don't know the names of any of the other Jews who were carried into exile and put into the service of the king of Babylon, only these four boys who had decided to remain pure from the first day they arrived in Babylon.

What about us? Will we remain pure?

In the seemingly hopeless pagan society we find ourselves in, this is the first commitment we need to make:

I resolve to avoid personal moral defilement.

Chapter 3
Now is the Time to Worship
Daniel 2

What's It All About?

Daniel chapters 2 and 3 are often seen as separate stories, but they are really two parts of the same story. Their focus is often seen to be Daniel's remarkable interpretation of Nebuchadnezzar's dream, or Hananiah, Mishael and Azariah's remarkable deliverance from the fiery furnace. But that misses the point of the dream and of the story of these two chapters. The focus of these chapters is not on human beings at all, but on the nature of God. In fact, Daniel clearly stated that the point of the dream was not to prove Daniel's interpretive powers but to reveal God's plan for the world (Daniel 2:30).

Pagan Religion

Nebuchadnezzar had a dream which troubled him. So he called in his magicians, enchanters, sorcerers and astrologers. And when they could not interpret his dream, he decreed that all of the "wise men," including administrators such as Daniel, Hananiah, Mishael and Azariah, would be executed. In essence, Nebuchadnezzar blamed the entire intellectual class for the failure of his astrologers. We may find this strange since we separate religion and science, but for the Babylonians all branches of knowledge were inextricably intertwined. When Daniel and his friends were trained in "the language and literature of the Babylonians" (Daniel 1:4), the curriculum would have included teaching about astrology and the magic arts. The god Nebo (also spelled Nabu), the son of Bel/Marduk, after whom Abednego was renamed (and after whom Nebuchadnezzar was named as well), was said to be the god of science, astronomy and writing. Fundamental to Babylonian knowledge were the secret arts of the magicians, enchanters, sorcerers and astrologers, the rituals and tricks which these practitioners could use to manipulate and coerce the gods into doing what human beings wanted. Because the gods were limited, they could be fooled and bribed. The science of agriculture involved methods of convincing the sky god to send rain. Medicine involved methods of driving away the spirits that caused illness.

Nor were religion and politics separate. The city of Babylon was said to have been founded by the god Marduk—possibly another name for Nimrod, the great hunter who founded the city (Genesis 10:8-10) and was later raised to the status of being a god. When the king was crowned, he was said to be "taking the hand of Bel," another name for Marduk. The king also functioned as the chief priest (perhaps in the same way that the king or queen of England is considered the head of the Church of England).

Altogether, the Babylonians worshiped hundreds of gods. They saw spirits everywhere and lived in fear of them. The gods were immoral, cruel, limited in their power and indifferent to the fate of human beings. With all of their failings, these gods seem very similar to people, but with slightly more power, something like modern comic book superheroes. Babylon, in the plain of Shinar, is thought to be the location of the Tower of Babel, where human beings united to worship their own power and achievements—until the true God came down, confused their language and defeated their efforts (Genesis 11:1-9).

In the Babylonian religious system, dreams were considered significant, a communication from the gods that needed to be interpreted by the religious experts, the magicians, enchanters, sorcerers and astrologers.

Nebuchadnezzar's demand that the sorcerers first tell him the dream and then the interpretation was a violation of the religious norms. As the gods were limited, so were the powers of the sorcerers who claimed to be allied with the gods. The sorcerers rightly protested that the king was demanding too much. Nebuchadnezzar thus comes across as an arbitrary and arrogant tyrant who was abusing his power. There is no doubt that Nebuchadnezzar was arrogant and tyrannical. But he was no fool. He was an extremely competent ruler. His father Nabopolasser had re-established Babylon as an independent kingdom, overthrowing the Assyrian Empire, but it was Nebuchadnezzar who made Babylon a great empire. Even while his father was still alive, it was Nebuchadnezzar who had led the armies which crushed the Egyptian army, invaded Palestine and extended Babylonian rule to the borders of Egypt. It was also Nebuchadnezzar who rebuilt the city of Babylon itself, including the great Processional Way, the temples and palaces and the wonderful hanging gardens.

Nebuchadnezzar was arrogant, but he was highly intelligent. As an insider, he had begun to question the validity of the Babylonian religious system. He had begun to suspect that the sorcerers were fakes. They could offer him an interpretation of his dream alright, but how would he know if the interpretation was correct? How could he know that the sorcerers were receiving their interpretation from the gods and weren't just making up an interpretation on their own? The sorcerers would probably be long dead before the interpretation could be proven by later history to be correct or incorrect. Nebuchadnezzar had not forgotten his dream, and he used that knowledge to arrange a test of the sorcerers' power. He decided that if they could tell him what the dream was, then he would know that the gods really were revealing information to the sorcerers and that the sorcerers' interpretation of the dream might also come from the gods. It was quite clever on Nebuchadnezzar's part. In response, the sorcerers admitted that they really did not have much actual religious knowledge. They said, "What the king asks is too difficult. No one can reveal it to the king except the gods, and they do not live among humans" (Daniel 2:11).

These "wise men" were very similar to modern psychics. My daughter tuned in to her favorite radio talk show one day only to discover to her dismay that a psychic was the guest. Listeners were invited to phone in, state their names and ask questions. My daughter commented, "If the psychic really knew things, why would people have to state their names and ask their questions? Shouldn't a psychic know these things?"

Responding to a Crisis

Daniel and his friends became involved in this matter because Nebuchadnezzar ordered that they were to be executed along with all the other intellectuals because of the failure of the sorcerers to interpret the dream. This was terribly unfair because they had had no part in the outlandish claims made by the sorcerers, as Jews they had been taught to never have anything to do with sorcery (Deuteronomy 18:9-13) and they had had no opportunity to interpret the dream. When told he was about to be executed, Daniel didn't know anything about the matter.

It is amazing that Daniel could act with such grace in this extremely difficult situation. He did not react with anger or fear as almost anyone else would have done. Instead of panicking, he took several practical steps to deal with the situation.

First, Daniel talked "with wisdom and tact" to the man who had come to kill him—a remarkable approach (Daniel 2:14-15). He decided, quite rightly, that the first thing to do was to find out exactly what the problem was. It is always a good idea to do research and think through a problem before acting.

Second, Daniel asked for an extension of the deadline (Daniel 2:16). This was a reasonable request, although one the sorcerers had not thought of. Given his anger and his arrogance, it is a bit surprising that Nebuchadnezzar agreed to the extension. He had already accused the sorcerers of stalling (2:8). But he was a very competent ruler, and he was wise enough to know that he wanted an interpretation of his dream more than he wanted revenge on the sorcerers. It might also be that God directly intervened to soften the king's answer. In asking for an extension, Daniel was using a similar approach to the one he had used in chapter 1. He asked the authorities for a grace period rather than seeing the authorities as the enemy. Daniel's success in using this technique in the first chapter might have given him confidence to try it again here in an even more dangerous situation.

Third, Daniel explained the problem to his friends and prayed with them for a solution (Daniel 2:17-18). When things go wrong, it is very easy to become angry with God and stop talking to Him. Daniel and his friends, however, responded with faith in God. This, I think, is the source of Daniel's remarkable grace in responding to the crisis. Instead of focusing on the problems, Daniel kept his focus on God— and a very different God from the ones the Babylonians worshiped. Like Peter walking on water (Matthew 14:22-33), we can do remarkable things as long as we keep looking at Jesus instead of looking at the wind and the waves. In fact, Daniel's focus on God and his trust in God were so great that he was able to go to bed and sleep rather than spending the night in fear—and this provided the opportunity for God to answer Daniel's prayer.

The God Who Answers

When I have taught the book of Daniel in Bible classes and care groups and asked what the key thought is in chapter 2, a common response is that God "reveals deep and hidden things" (Daniel 2:22). We are bottom line people. The important thing, we think, is that God revealed the dream and so saved Daniel and his friends. That is as human-centered as the approach of the Babylonians. But the real focus here is on God's glory, not on Daniel's safety.

With the benefit of hindsight, we say that of course God revealed the dream to Daniel, but Daniel was not so sure this would happen. Daniel seems to have been quite confident that God *could* interpret the dream, but whether He *would* do so was entirely up to Him. Unlike the sorcerers, Daniel did not try to trick or manipulate his God. Such tactics are useless with the God of Heaven. Rather, Daniel and his friends simply pleaded for mercy (Daniel 2:18), an approach that acknowledged that God has all power, that humans have no claim on God's miracles or revelation and that God has complete sovereignty to act in whatever way He wants to. And when God did answer with a full revelation, Daniel took time to respond with a song of thanks and praise (Daniel 2:19-23). Furthermore, when it came time to explain the dream to Nebuchadnezzar, Daniel was careful to explain that the interpretation did not come from his own ability (in contrast to the sorcerers, who claimed special powers and insights). Rather, he gave full credit for the interpretation to God (Daniel 2:27-28). It was God who *chose* to provide knowledge to Nebuchadnezzar. Daniel could take no credit for convincing God or tricking God or bribing God into providing answers. Daniel's God does not operate the way the pagan gods did.

In contrast to the pagan gods, who were limited in their powers and who were largely indifferent to human affairs (they "do not live among humans"—Daniel 2:11), it is interesting to look at Daniel's understanding of God.

Daniel did not mention the name "Yahweh," although it is clear this is the God he was referring to. In his praise, he mentioned "the name of God" (Daniel 2:20) and the "God of my ancestors" (Daniel 2:23). It is important to note that, starting with Daniel 2:4, this book is written "in Aramaic," the language used by the Babylonian Empire, and so Daniel used words that Nebuchadnezzar and other Babylonians would understand. To Nebuchadnezzar, he referred to "the God of heaven" (Daniel 2:18,19,28,37,44) and "the great God" (Daniel 2:45). Daniel went on to state that the God of Heaven controls nature (Daniel 2:21,38). Although Daniel did not state this here, it is clear that he was basing his statements on the biblical teaching that Yahweh is the Creator of everything. Daniel had read Genesis 1. Daniel also stated that it is Yahweh who controls human destiny. It is Yahweh who raises up empires and gives kings their power (Daniel 2:21,37-38,44-45). Yahweh is not only all-powerful, but He deliberately, continually and systematically intervenes in the lives of human beings. This is again in sharp contrast to the pagan gods, who were often indifferent to human beings, who had to be persuaded to intervene and whose involvement was inconsistent. Nebuchadnezzar neatly summarized what Daniel had said by affirming that the God of Heaven is "the God of gods and the Lord of kings" (Daniel 2:47).

Daniel also described God as "the revealer of mysteries" (Daniel 2:28-30), a term that Nebuchadnezzar also picked up (Daniel 2:47). Daniel further said that God had deliberately chosen to show King Nebuchadnezzar what He was going to do. The dream wasn't an accident, a "leak" from God's government. In his song of praise, Daniel explained further that God "gives wisdom to the wise and knowledge to the discerning. He reveals deep and hidden things; he knows what lies in darkness, and light dwells with him" (Daniel 2:21-22). Specifically, Daniel said that Yahweh had revealed the meaning of Nebuchadnezzar's dream to Daniel (Daniel 2:23,30). This is a fundamental and tremendously significant point. Knowledge is power. The pagan gods and sorcerers fiercely guarded their limited amounts of secret knowledge. The God of Heaven has unlimited power and knowledge and has no need to do so. He is the God of light and revelation. God's intention is not that people should remain in ignorance and confusion. From the beginning of time, God has been revealing truth to humanity—through Moses, through

Daniel, through the Bible and finally through His ultimate revelation, Jesus Christ. God does not deal in mysteries (a pagan term for secret knowledge which is limited to the select few). God deals in revelation. That is why He sent a dream to Nebuchadnezzar, the ruler of the most significant empire on earth, and why He sent Daniel to Nebuchadnezzar's court to interpret it for him. God wanted Nebuchadnezzar and everyone in his vast empire to know the truth. That might be the main reason God gave Nebuchadnezzar such a vast empire to begin with.

What set Daniel and his friends apart from everyone else in this story is that they understood the nature of God. They had read and believed God's declaration at the beginning of the Ten Commandments: "I am the LORD [Yahweh] your God, who brought you out of Egypt, out of the land of slavery. You shall have no other gods before me" (Exodus 20:2-3). Daniel and his friends were the only ones in this story who knew God and were able to see things from God's perspective.

The Vision

Daniel then correctly related to Nebuchadnezzar the dream that he had had. He had seen a great statue with four parts, a head of gold, a chest of silver, an abdomen of bronze, and legs and feet of iron and clay (or brick). The statue was evidently in the shape of a man (implying that the dream had something to do with human beings). Then a great rock smashed the statue and ground it to powder. Before we turn to the interpretation, we should note the remarkable fact that this was evidently the same dream that Nebuchadnezzar had had. The chances of two people having exactly the same dream are very remote. This demonstrates clearly that this was not just a dream like other dreams people have. It was, in fact, a vision given to both men by the God who controls nature and human affairs—and even the thoughts in humans' minds.

Because Daniel had correctly related the dream, Nebuchadnezzar must now have been hopeful that Daniel could also provide the interpretation. The dream had seemed significant to him, so significant and so troubling that he couldn't sleep (Daniel 2:1). Was it a prediction? A warning? A promise? An instruction that needed to be followed? While he certainly didn't know the full interpretation, it is possible that Nebuchadnezzar might have already guessed that the dream had something to do with himself and his kingdom.

Then Daniel explained the dream. The statue, he said, represented four "kingdoms," really four great empires. The statue was "enormous," "dazzling" and "awesome" (Daniel 2:31). These were not ordinary kingdoms. From our vantage point, it is very easy to identify these empires (even if we didn't have the help of Daniel's dream of the four beasts in Daniel 7-8 and the interpretation of that dream that God sent him through an angel). From the vantage point of history, we can readily see that these empires were the Babylonian Empire (626-539 BC); the Persian Empire (539-331 BC); the Greek Empire achieved briefly by Alexander the Great (331-323 BC) but whose influence continued for centuries afterward; and the Roman Empire (146 BC-476 AD). The description even includes the fact that the Roman Empire was eventually divided in two, a division that persists today in the distinction between eastern and western Europe (just as the two arms might suggest that the Persian Empire was led by two nations, the Medes and the Persians). In fact, this description of the four empires, written at the beginning of the first of the four empires, was so accurate that later skeptics have had to go to great lengths to explain away the remarkable accuracy of God's prophecy. The skeptics do not believe in a God who controls history and reveals mysteries. Therefore, they insist, without any evidence, that the book of Daniel must have been written much later, in the second century BC. But even that late a date was long before the Roman Empire conquered the eastern half of the Mediterranean and certainly long before the Roman Empire was divided.

It is interesting that the description of the empires follows the same pattern as the development of metal technology, although at a later date. The softer but more valuable metals, gold and silver, were refined first. Then, as technology developed hotter smelting fires, humans were able to refine bronze (a mixture of copper and tin) and then iron. The Bronze Age in the Middle East generally lasted from about 3000 to 1200 BC and was followed by the Iron Age. Iron is a good metaphor for the Roman Empire, which was far less culturally sophisticated but stronger and more practical than its predecessors. Rome was not mainly famous for its art or literature, which it mostly borrowed from the Greeks, but for its army, roads, water and sewer systems and administrative skill. We are so convinced of the myth of progress, perhaps even influenced by the theory of evolution, that we believe the tendency of history is to constant improvement. What the image of the statue suggests is not progress, but decline. The history of human kingdoms is winding down.

The most remarkable aspect of the dream, however, is not the description of the statue, the amazingly accurate prophecy of the four empires, but the description of the rock that destroyed them. Statues are made of metal refined from rock by human beings. Thus the statue, representing human kingdoms, was made of metal and shaped like a human being. But in the dream these kingdoms were destroyed and replaced by a rock, cut out of a mountain "not by human hands" (Daniel 2:34-45). This rock, as Daniel explained, represents a new kingdom, not a kingdom established by human beings but a kingdom established by God. It is the Kingdom of God established by God's Son, Jesus Christ, during the time of the Roman Empire, as the dream so accurately predicted. God in the Old Testament was often described as a "rock" (Psalm 18:2, Isaiah 26:4 and many other verses), a term denoting strength and refuge. Jesus was also described as a rock (Romans 9:33, 1 Corinthians 10:4), and Jesus said that He would build His church on a rock, His apostle Peter and the faith that Peter had expressed (Matthew 16:13-19).

The Purpose and Meaning of the Dream

Human beings are often very self-centered and narrow-minded. Reading the story today, we focus on Daniel and his friends, and we marvel at how God answered prayer and revealed the dream to save Daniel and his friends from execution. We take hope from that that God will similarly rescue us from our difficulties. Daniel did not have such a narrow view. He knew that in the grand scheme of things, his own life was unimportant. Daniel looked at the whole episode from the perspective of why the dream came in the first place and what God was doing. The dream didn't come to save Daniel and his friends. Daniel understood that the dream had been sent as a revelation to Nebuchadnezzar and everyone else in his vast empire (Daniel 2:30) and indeed the billions of people in future history who would read the book of Daniel.

What was the revelation? In the first place, it was a revelation of God Himself. God wanted to teach Nebuchadnezzar that He was Yahweh, the God revealed through the people of Israel, the God who created and controls the natural world and the world of human beings, the God who raises up and destroys human kingdoms, the God who reveals the truth.

Second, God wanted to teach Nebuchadnezzar that it was He who had given Nebuchadnezzar his power and that He had given that power for a specific reason (Daniel 2:36-38). God wanted to teach Nebuchadnezzar that He was not only the God who rules human affairs, but also the God who had His hand on Nebuchadnezzar's life, the God who wanted to have a personal relationship with him, the God who wanted to make Nebuchadnezzar His servant.

Third, God wanted to tell Nebuchadnezzar (and everyone else who would read about the dream) about the coming Kingdom of Jesus Christ. The dream was sent to proclaim the gospel, the good news of Jesus, to the whole world. As we shall see, Nebuchadnezzar did not get it, at least not then. Having been told that the great kingdoms of the world would be replaced by the far greater Kingdom of God, that the nations are as dust on God's scales (Isaiah 40, especially verses 15-17), he still chose in the next chapter to set up a gold statue and compel people to worship him.

It's Our Turn

This chapter challenges us in at least three areas.

First, we should ask ourselves whom we are worshiping. We may say that we are Christians and that we worship the "Christian God." But is that really true? Are we sure we have a fully biblical view of God? The God revealed in the Bible is the sovereign Creator who controls everything, knows everything, is perfectly holy and loves human beings. He can't be fooled, bribed or manipulated. Yet it is very easy for us to fall into the habit of thinking of Him as a lesser god. We may find ourselves thinking that God doesn't really know or care about the sins we commit, including the evil thoughts in our heads and hearts. We may think He will overlook our sins if we give some extra money to the church. We may bargain with Him, promising to give up some sin or perform some good deed if God will just make sure that we get that promotion at work or heal our child. We may go about our daily business as if God does not "live among humans" (Daniel 2:11), as if He does not want to be intimately involved in all aspects of our lives. We may forget that He is the holy God who has called us to holy living and commanded that we worship only Him. We may be unsure of the fact that God is the unparalleled revealer of mysteries, thinking that His revelation is on the same level as the uninformed speculation of other religions. This story challenges us to again recognize who the true God really is.

Second, this chapter challenges us on how we respond in a crisis. Difficult situations are tests that reveal our inner reality. When faced with trouble, opposition, sickness or death, our first response is often fear or anger, maybe even panic. Yet, if we have a deep trust in God like Daniel's, we should be able to remain calm, investigate the problem, take practical steps, refuse to see other people as the enemy and pray. We can remain faithful to the true God even if the situation does not turn out well. We really can. But will we?

Third, this chapter challenges us on whether our focus is truly on the Kingdom of God. Before we are too quick to criticize Nebuchadnezzar, we should stand back and consider our own failings. Too often when we modern Christians turn to the book of Daniel, we do so to find out what will happen to the great empires of the earth, the King of the North and the King of the South, the possibly revived Roman Empire, the Beast and the Antichrist. We miss the main point of the vision God gave to Nebuchadnezzar and to us. The revelation of the empires ends with the Roman Empire. There is no mention of the British Empire or the United States or any other modern nation. Since the coming of Jesus two thousand years ago, the kingdoms of the earth no longer matter. They have been ground to dust. The only kingdom we need concern ourselves with is the Kingdom of God, the remarkable inheritance given to us in Jesus Christ. No wonder Nebuchadnezzar didn't get it looking forward. We who call ourselves Christians often don't get it either, even with the benefit of further revelation and the advantage of looking back. We have been given the keys to the Kingdom of Heaven, and too often we are concerned with building our own puny kingdoms instead. We have been granted a vision of God's purpose for all of humanity, and too often we are preoccupied with our own survival, on what's in it for us.

Chapter 4
Now is the Time to Worship (Part 2)
Daniel 3

He Just Doesn't Get It

This chapter, like the previous one, demands that we think about the nature of God. It again reveals the varying viewpoints that people have about God.

Let's begin with Nebuchadnezzar. Chapter 2 ended with him declaring that Daniel's God is "the God of gods and the Lord of kings and a revealer of mysteries" (Daniel 2:47). He had been given a remarkable vision of the character of God and of the coming Kingdom of Heaven, and God had sent Daniel to explain it all to him. We might expect that as a result of all this he would have had an adequate understanding of God.

But he didn't.

The point of the vision that had been given to Nebuchadnezzar was that earthly kingdoms, as great as they are, are dust in comparison to the Kingdom of God, that kings and emperors, as powerful as they seem, are only pawns in the hands of God, raised up and replaced at His command. But Nebuchadnezzar didn't get it. His vision was firmly fixed on himself, and it would take more than a first lesson to get him to move. All Nebuchadnezzar took away from the vision was that his own empire was the greatest of them all, being composed of gold, and that he was the greatest king of all.

So he set up a gold statue ninety feet high. The statue was probably a representation of Nebuchadnezzar himself—like one of the great stone statues of one of the Egyptian Pharaohs. Having been given a vision of the great God of Heaven, Nebuchadnezzar chose to worship himself. How foolish! But how human!

Nebuchadnezzar's statue was ninety feet high and nine feet wide. Even if it was only gold-plated and not solid gold, the amount of gold required to build such a statue would have been enormous. This is an indication of Nebuchadnezzar's great wealth and power. Yet it is still true that his wealth and power were as nothing compared to the wealth and power of the true God who created it all. Literally, the original text says Nebuchadnezzar built a statue sixty cubits high and six cubits wide, a cubit being a unit of measurement equal to about a foot and a half. The unit of measurement doesn't matter. However, it is interesting to note that in biblical terms six is the number of human beings—since human beings were created on the sixth day (Genesis 1:24-31). The book of Revelation describes an anti-Christian "beast" who will set up a statue and compel people to worship it (Revelation 13:11-18). Revelation says that this beast has a number, which is "man's number," 666, and that people will be required to have this number on their right hands or foreheads if they want to buy and sell. Both parts of the Bible, the Old and New Testaments, refer to the common human tendency to worship ourselves rather than God. This was the original sin in the Garden of Eden, when human beings tried to put themselves in the place of God (Genesis 3:5). So, Nebuchadnezzar built a statue of himself. He built it all of gold, even though he knew from his dream and should have known from his own experience that human beings are not pure but have feet of clay, that they are powerless whenever they encounter the real God. It should be noted in passing that Nebuchadnezzar's beautiful, expensive statue has long since disappeared. Other than its mention in Daniel 3, there is no longer even a record of it.

Yet Nebuchadnezzar did not realize all this. Having built the statue, he then commanded that all of the leaders of his vast empire fall down and worship this great statue of himself. It is interesting to note that even before anyone had refused, Nebuchadnezzar threatened to kill anyone who did not worship him. The furnace was probably not erected as a punishment chamber but was probably the smelting furnace that had been used to refine the gold for the statue. Nebuchadnezzar ordered that it be heated seven times hotter than usual, perhaps implying that Nebuchadnezzar had kept a fire burning in the furnace just in case. This suggests that Nebuchadnezzar knew that unless they were coerced, people would not worship his statue, that deep down he knew he wasn't a god worthy of worship. But he insisted anyway. The fascinating thing is that the true God does not do that—He simply reveals Himself and expects that people will recognize His greatness and *choose* to worship Him. He does not force us to worship Him. And even at the end of this chapter, when Nebuchadnezzar had seen again the greatness of the true God, he still operated as if he was in charge, as if he could control his people's religious beliefs. He commanded everyone in his empire to respect the God of the Jews, just as he had tried to compel them to worship his statue. He still didn't get it. He did not realize that God did not need his help and that the true God would continue to invite, not force, people to worship Him.

Nebuchadnezzar's real problem was not that he was unable to assess his own power, but that he still did not know God and understand His power. Even though he had been granted a glimpse of the real God, he was still committed to worshiping the false Babylonian gods (Daniel 3:12,14). Since the gods that he worshiped were limited, he assumed that the true God, Yahweh, was also limited. He essentially declared that once Hananiah, Mishael and Azariah were thrown into the fire, no god could save them (Daniel 3:15). None of the gods Nebuchadnezzar worshiped could raise people from the dead, and he didn't expect the God of the Jews could do so either. It is never a wise decision to challenge Almighty God.

The Wise Men

The overlooked characters in this drama are the astrologers (Daniel 3:8-12). Yet they are real people, and they deserve some of our attention. These astrologers were some of the wise men, the people who had previously offered what they had claimed was divine wisdom and guidance to the king. They were thus among the men who had failed so miserably to interpret the king's dream in chapter 2. They were also among the men whose lives had been saved by Daniel's successful interpretation of the dream.

We should be clear that only "some" astrologers accused Hananiah, Mishael and Azariah. We do not know what the other astrologers and wise men thought. But we do know what these men thought, and their thoughts were evil. One might have expected them to be grateful to Daniel and his friends for saving their lives. But they were not. Presumably they were consumed by jealousy over Daniel's successful interpretation and over the promotions Daniel and his friends had received. Probably they hoped that Nebuchadnezzar would reward them for their worship of him and their act of informing on those who refused to worship him. Perhaps they hoped to return to the position of trusted advisors to the king once Daniel and his friends were out of the way. Perhaps they coveted the administrative posts which would be vacant once Hananiah, Mishael and Azariah were dead. Their act of betrayal and ingratitude strikes us as evil, but it must be remembered that the gods they worshiped were also cruel, self-serving and devious. It is said that we become like the gods we worship. In spite of the modern tendency to think that all religions are alike, it is only Yahweh who is a righteous and holy God and who demands holy living from His followers.

There is something else. Along with Nebuchadnezzar, these astrologers had had an opportunity to see the true God at work. They had seen that the God of the Jews was more powerful than their gods, that He revealed truth while their gods dealt in darkness and obscurity. It is a sad fact that these men had closed minds and that they chose to reject the obvious truth and cling to what was not true. It was not lack of evidence, but lack of willingness to accept the evidence. How sad. And how human.

Hananiah, Mishael and Azariah

Daniel does not seem to have been present at this worship service for Nebuchadnezzar. If he had been there and had worshiped the statue, someone (the astrologers, Daniel's three friends or Nebuchadnezzar) would surely have mentioned it. If he had been there and hadn't worshiped the statue, he would have been in the furnace with his friends. The Bible does not explain why Daniel was not present. Possibly, he held such a high position in the government that he could be excused. Perhaps he was away on business. Daniel's unexplained absence is an indication that the Bible is not a book about people like Daniel but a book about God. It does not matter that Daniel was not present. What matters is that God was.

Daniel was not present, but Hananiah, Mishael and Azariah were, and Nebuchadnezzar's command presented them with a major dilemma.

Picture the situation. It was a massive public ceremony, staged on the plain of Dura. We don't know where that was exactly, but it was obviously a large flat area, capable of accommodating thousands of people. The crowd was so large that the act of defiance by Hananiah, Mishael and Azariah was not seen by Nebuchadnezzar and his officials, and it might have gone unnoticed if the astrologers had not informed on them. There was an orchestra, probably a large orchestra so that it could be heard at the back of the crowd, there being no electronic sound systems in those days. There were soldiers and probably organizers. Nearby was the smelting furnace where the gold for the statue had been refined. King

Nebuchadnezzar was probably sitting on a raised throne, dressed in his royal robes, perhaps under a canopy to protect him from the sun, surrounded by courtiers. It was a celebration of Nebuchadnezzar's power, a day for pomp and ceremony. And towering over it all, gleaming in the sun, was that magnificent golden statue.

Bowing before a golden statue was clearly something that worshipers of the true God, Yahweh, should not do. Every Jewish boy would know of the covenant which God had given to Israel after He had overpowered the gods of Egypt and delivered the nation from slavery: "I am the LORD [Yahweh] your God, who brought you out of Egypt, out of the land of slavery. You shall have no other gods before me. You shall not make for yourself an image in the form of anything in heaven above or on the earth beneath or in the waters below. You shall not bow down to them or worship them" (Exodus 20:2-5). Yet, just as in chapter 1, Hananiah, Mishael and Azariah could have found many excuses to go along with the crowd. They had just been placed in positions of influence, places where they could start doing some real good in the world, and they could have considered that it would be a shame to throw their lives away now. They could have told themselves that this was just a public formality, an unpleasant but necessary part of their jobs, a demonstration of loyalty to their employer, and that it didn't really mean they were worshiping Nebuchadnezzar or the gods he was said to represent. Looking over that vast crowd of important officials from all over the empire, they could surely have used the excuse that "everybody's doing it," probably including other Jewish exiles in the king's service. In that vast crowd, who would even notice or care what they did?

And yet Hananiah, Mishael and Azariah chose to remain faithful to the true God. They refused to worship Nebuchadnezzar's golden idol, just as they had chosen to refuse idol-tainted meat in chapter 1. The stakes were higher this time. They had a higher profile for one thing. They were important officials, not just some ignorant slave boys. More was expected of them. This was also a far more public occasion; the king's honor would demand that what could be overlooked in the cafeteria could not be overlooked on a public stage. And worshiping an idol was a more clear-cut violation of Yahweh's commands than failing to observe dietary regulations. This was a major test. Yet it is probably true that if the three friends had not chosen to be faithful on the minor issue in chapter 1, they would not have had the courage to be faithful now.

From our position of hindsight, we think the choice was easy because we know that God protected Hananiah, Mishael and Azariah. They had no such assurance. It is instructive to observe their response to the situation. Brought before the king, they did not deny their actions or excuse them or plead for mercy. They were calm and respectful to the king. But they did not waver. Just like Daniel in chapter 2, they knew that their God was able to protect them, but they had no assurance that He would. After all, they knew many thousands of their fellow Jews had been slaughtered by Babylonian troops. Yet they chose to remain faithful to God. They were willing to die for their faith.

Why were Hananiah, Mishael and Azariah able to meet this challenge? The answer is that, alone of all the people there, they knew God. They were absolutely convinced that Yahweh was more powerful than Nebuchadnezzar and his thousands of soldiers. They knew that Yahweh was far more worthy of worship than this tyrant of a king. They also knew that Nebuchadnezzar's power was temporary and transitory, that in a few years or decades it would be only a memory, but that they served the eternal God who had promised them a kingdom that would last forever. They believed in the God who is able to save, the God who is sovereign and cannot be manipulated, the God who can be trusted no matter what. Once you have come to know the real God, the pale substitutes no longer have any appeal. Regardless of the difficulty of the immediate situation, from the perspective of eternity the decision was easy.

So Hananiah, Mishael and Azariah were thrown into the smelting furnace, probably from the top, where the fuel and raw ore were poured in (since they "fell" into the furnace: Daniel 3:23). This refining fire killed their executioners, but destroyed only their bonds. After this, the three friends were free. They had faced their worst fears, they had faced death, and now, whatever else happened in their lives, they should never be troubled by doubt and fear again. The wise men of Babylon had declared that the gods "do not live among humans" (Daniel 2:11). Hananiah, Mishael and Azariah had believed differently. Now they knew for sure. In the midst of the fire, they were joined by one who looked like "a son of the gods" (Daniel 3:25), probably a pre-incarnate appearance of Jesus Christ, God Himself. What a wonderful privilege! It was an experience they would remember all their lives. And yet they would have missed out on it if they had not refused to worship the golden idol of Nebuchadnezzar. Renewed and blessed, they walked out of the bottom of the furnace, where the refined gold flowed out.

Nations and Peoples of Every Language

Nebuchadnezzar set up his statue on the plain of Dura in the province of Babylon (Daniel 3:1), which would be the central province of an empire composed of many provinces. Then he "summoned the satraps, prefects, governors, advisors, treasurers, judges, magistrates and all the other provincial officials" (Daniel 3:2-3). While a wide range of officials seem to have been summoned (from the judiciary to the finance department and not just the top officials), this seems to imply that these officials were only from the province of Babylon. However, in verse 4, they were addressed as "nations and peoples of every language." Although there were certainly people of many nations in the king's service in Babylon (including the Jewish exiles), this seems to imply something larger. The fact that the astrologers identified Hananiah, Mishael and Azariah as being from the province of Babylon (Daniel 3:12) also suggests that the crowd was drawn from a larger area. It is quite possible that Nebuchadnezzar had planned a much larger gathering, summoning his officials from all over the empire. Given the length of time that travel took in those days, some officials would have had to stay behind to keep the empire running during the months that the trip would take, but there is no reason to think that Nebuchadnezzar could not have summoned such a large group. It would be in keeping with his personality to want to be worshiped by as many people as possible. The point of the whole exercise was to demonstrate his own greatness and power.

What is interesting to observe is that the occasion Nebuchadnezzar had planned in order to demonstrate his own power, instead ended up being an occasion that demonstrated the power of Yahweh, the one true God. The vast crowd of leaders Nebuchadnezzar had summoned instead witnessed God delivering Hananiah, Mishael and Azariah from the furnace, crowding around them to see this miracle for themselves (Daniel 3:27). What Daniel and his friends had understood and explained was that the great God was all-powerful, setting up and using kings and emperors for His own ends. This had now been amply demonstrated. These leaders of society had seen the miracle of the furnace, they had received the emperor's command to respect Israel's God, and they would carry this message to the far corners of the empire. One can imagine the impact of their story when they got back home. None of this would have been possible if the Jews had successfully fought off the Babylonian invasion. Yahweh is indeed "the Most High God" (Daniel 3:26), a title He had received earlier from non-Jewish peoples (Genesis 14:18-19), and He will be worshiped to the ends of the earth.

Modern Questions

The question of who God is and the question of whom or what we should worship were not settled 2,600 years ago. The questions that Hananiah, Mishael and Azariah faced are the same questions we face today.

There is the temptation of *syncretism*, the idea that we can follow several religions at once, that we can call ourselves Christians and go to church but look to some other source for direction and comfort. Some "Christians," for instance, read horoscopes for their daily guidance. Others find comfort in transcendental meditation, which involves chanting the name of a Hindu god. Others may find their identity and highest purpose in cheering for a sports team or worshiping a musician who is their "idol." Such people embody the philosophy of the pagan emperor in this chapter. Nebuchadnezzar had already praised the God of the Jews. He did not mind if the Jews followed their religion—as long as they followed his as well. But religions conflict, the true God will not share our allegiance with any lesser power, and we have to make a choice.

Related to this is the temptation of *pluralism*, the idea that all religions are the same and it does not matter which religion we follow. This simply is not true. Religions are not all the same. Muslims do not believe in a personal relationship with God nor in forgiveness. Hindus believe in many gods. Buddhists aren't sure there is a God, just a vague life force that permeates the universe. Pagan religions believe the gods are immoral. Religions aren't all the same.

There is the temptation of *humanism*, the idea that human beings are the purpose and center and judge of life. In this understanding, human beings decide what is right and wrong. We do something if "it feels good to me." This often includes a large element of selfishness. We are encouraged to seek "self-fulfillment" or "personal satisfaction."

Related to this is the temptation of *nationalism*, the idea that our nation is the highest good and its laws and demands should overrule all others. This temptation arises when we are asked to do or support something immoral for the good of our nation, to put our nation ahead of God's commands to be holy. This is especially a temptation in the United States, which has traditionally been identified as a Christian nation. It is easy for Americans to assume that the United States and the Kingdom of God are synonymous. They are not. The American people are a mixture of Christians and pagans, highly moral and grossly immoral people. Like all other nations, sometimes the United States is on the side of truth, justice and mercy, but sometimes it acts with injustice and greed.

Even among North Americans who claim to be Christian, many have a sub-Christian understanding of God. They claim to worship the Christian God, but think of Him as immoral, tolerant of sin, remote and/or limited in His power.

We need to become reacquainted with the God of the Bible. Yahweh is the all-powerful God who created the universe and human beings, the God who daily sustains and controls the universe, the God who directs the history of human beings, overruling powerful kings and great empires and thwarting all human efforts to manipulate Him. Yahweh is the holy and moral God who gave us the Ten Commandments and insists that human beings also be holy and just. Other religions think that God does not live among human beings (Daniel 2:11), but the God of the Bible walked with Hananiah, Mishael and Azariah in the fiery furnace. Jesus is Immanuel (Matthew 1:23, Isaiah 7:14), which means "God with us," and He wants to have a personal relationship with every human being.

In the face of these challenges, Hananiah, Mishael and Azariah made a conscious decision, a deliberate commitment to worship only the true God (Daniel 3:18,28). We should do the same. In the seemingly hopeless pagan society we find ourselves in, this is the second commitment we need to make:

I will worship only the true God, even at the cost of my life.

Chapter 5
You Can Make a Difference
Daniel 4

A Question to Ponder

If you are a Christian, someone who is committed to the God of the Bible, you have the assurance that you will one day go to heaven to live with God in joy and peace and love forever. Now here is an interesting question: When you get there, which of these two might you expect to meet—Zedekiah, the last king of the remnant of God's chosen people, the Jews, or Nebuchadnezzar, the cruel, arrogant, pagan king of the pagan Babylonian Empire, named after a pagan god, the man who had conquered the Jews and destroyed Jerusalem, including the temple of God? The answer seems obvious. Yet, as we have seen earlier in the book of Daniel, there is much here that can change our perspective.

The Form

Daniel chapter 4 has an unusual form. We often think that a Bible book is like a modern book, written by a single author and telling a single story. Yet this is not always true, and it is not true of the book of Daniel. The book of Daniel is a collection of documents. The first six chapters relate six different stories, spaced over almost 70 years (from 605 to about 539 or 538 BC), with wide gaps in between. The first four occurred during Nebuchadnezzar's long reign (605-562

BC). The book is not a biography of Daniel, but a relation of certain events which reveal the nature of God. The book is not about Daniel but about God. (There are apocryphal stories that people later attempted to add to the book of Daniel, but it is very obvious that they are additions that don't belong in Scripture because their purpose is to show off Daniel's wisdom, not God's.)

The first three chapters of Daniel seem to have occurred near the beginning of Nebuchadnezzar's reign. However, chapter 4 seems to have occurred toward the end of his reign—at least, this is what is implied by some other ancient documents which make vague references to the events recorded in chapter 4. (These documents need not concern us, but it is worth mentioning that they provide a little corroboration of the truth of the Bible's account.) In another sense, as far as Nebuchadnezzar is concerned, chapter 4 is the culmination of the story begun in chapters 1-3.

The first three chapters of Daniel are told in the third person, that is, by a narrator who was not any of the characters in the story. Who this narrator was we don't know. It has traditionally been assumed that it was Daniel, and this could well be true since the first chapters are bound together with the later chapters, which Daniel did write. The vividness and the detail certainly indicate that the author was someone who was present at the events he is describing. Chapter 4, however, starts out in the first person, with Nebuchadnezzar telling the story. In the middle of the chapter (verses 19-33), the story reverts to the third-person narrator, but then Nebuchadnezzar finishes the story at the end of the chapter. The parts by Nebuchadnezzar seem to be a royal proclamation or official statement issued by King Nebuchadnezzar. The intended audience was immense. The document was addressed not only to everyone in the Babylonian Empire but to everyone in the world (4:1). It would seem then that chapter 4 is a royal proclamation that Daniel incorporated into his book, which was then preserved by the Jews as part of their holy writings, the Old Testament part of the Bible.

But what about verses 19-33, those verses in the third person in the middle of the king's proclamation? There are several possibilities. First, it may be that the king's proclamation itself made the switch in voice, the scribe who wrote it (or the king who dictated it) getting confused by the dialogue between Daniel and the king and forgetting that the king was supposed to be narrating the whole document. Such errors occur in government documents and other documents all the time, especially when good editors are not present to make sure all the grammar is right. Another possibility is that Daniel replaced the middle part of the king's proclamation. Perhaps the king's version was too long or included information that Daniel considered irrelevant for his own purposes. Perhaps Daniel wanted to include some details that the king had left out. It doesn't greatly matter. The third-person part of the story in the middle is completely consistent with what was said in Nebuchadnezzar's proclamation at the beginning and end of the chapter.

A final comment about form. Near the beginning and again near the end of the proclamation, Nebuchadnezzar broke into poetry, offering essentially a hymn of praise to God. This is indicated by an ancient poetic device called parallelism, saying the same thing twice but with different words: "How great are his signs, how mighty his wonders!" (4:3). The next two parallel phrases "His kingdom is an eternal kingdom; his dominion endures from generation to generation" (4:3) are repeated at the end of the proclamation but with the words "kingdom" and "dominion" interchanged, achieving a kind of double parallelism: "His dominion is an eternal dominion; his kingdom endures from generation to generation" (4:34).

The Same Old Story

The parallels between chapter 4 and chapter 2 are also striking. Again Nebuchadnezzar had a troubling dream. Again he asked his "magicians, enchanters, astrologers and diviners" to interpret his dream, and again they could not do it. Again he turned to Daniel, who could interpret the dream because "the spirit of the holy gods is in him" (4:8-9,18). This description became a permanent part of Daniel's identity (5:11,14).

But there are also some differences. First, while the first dream "troubled" Nebuchadnezzar (2:1,3), this dream made him "afraid" and "terrified" (4:5,6). This may be because he already had a suspicion of what the dream was about and because this dream was much more personal. The enchanters might also have suspected the meaning of the dream but were afraid to say it. Indeed, even Daniel was reluctant to provide the interpretation (4:19-20). Second, this time Nebuchadnezzar did not bother to test Daniel or the enchanters by making them relate the dream as well as its interpretation. By now, Nebuchadnezzar was sure of Daniel's ability to interpret dreams. In that case, one wonders why he bothered to ask his enchanters first. Interpreting dreams was their job, while Daniel was more of an administrator, although all the wise men of Babylon were under his authority (2:48, 4:9, 5:11). Nebuchadnezzar also seems to have been a man who had trouble breaking away from the traditional Babylonian ways, a man bound by his traditional religion. The third difference is that there is no record of Daniel going away to pray and ask God for the interpretation in chapter 4 as there was in chapter 2. However, he did make clear that the interpretation came from God (4:24).

The relationship between Nebuchadnezzar and Daniel seems to have changed between chapter 2 and chapter 4. The two had no doubt spent many years working together because of Daniel's administrative position in the royal court (2:49). Nebuchadnezzar had come to trust and respect Daniel. It is remarkable that he might now have been willing to call Daniel by his own name rather than by the name he had tried to impose on him (4:8). That might also indicate that Nebuchadnezzar had developed a respect for Daniel's

God, for whom Daniel had originally been named, in comparison to the Babylonian gods, for whom he had been renamed. For his part, Daniel seems to have been genuinely distressed at the judgment that was about to fall on Nebuchadnezzar. He had grown to love this pagan king. They were now friends.

The Message of God

The message God was giving to Nebuchadnezzar was indeed frightful. It was not that the great empires of the earth would be replaced by the Kingdom of God. It was that Nebuchadnezzar himself would be deposed from his throne. It was one thing for Nebuchadnezzar to admit that Yahweh, the God of Heaven, was "the Lord of kings" (2:47) and an entirely different matter for Nebuchadnezzar to recognize the God of Heaven as Lord over Nebuchadnezzar himself. Now God's sovereignty was getting personal.

Nebuchadnezzar had two problems, according to Daniel. The first was Nebuchadnezzar's pride, his refusal to "acknowledge that the Most High is sovereign over all kingdoms on earth and gives them to anyone he wishes" (4:25,32). Instead, Nebuchadnezzar was convinced that his empire was "the great Babylon I have built...by my mighty power and for the glory of my majesty" (4:30). Despite the lesson in chapter 3, he was still building monuments to himself. Like many modern people, he was a self-made man who worshiped his creator. He was convinced that it was his own ability that had made him the most powerful man in the world. He thought royal power came to the most worthy, not "the lowliest of people" (4:17). Nebuchadnezzar's pride is understandable. He was the man who had led the armies that had expanded the Babylonian state into a great empire, the man who had built most of the great city of Babylon. The vision described Nebuchadnezzar as a tree in the middle of the land (4:10); Nebuchadnezzar dominated the civilized world; Babylon was the center of the world. The tree was described as "enormous," "large" and "strong" (4:10-11,20);

all of these are fitting descriptions of Nebuchadnezzar's power. The vision said that the tree's top "touched the sky" (4:11,20); Nebuchadnezzar was considered a god or at least one who "held the hand" of the god who had founded Babylon. The tree was "visible to the ends of the earth" (4:11,20); Nebuchadnezzar ruled an enormous empire, but his fame had surely spread beyond the borders of even that enormous empire. The tree had "beautiful leaves" (4:12,21); Nebuchadnezzar had all the trappings of royalty—gold and jewels and crowns and robes and thrones and palaces. Finally, the vision described Nebuchadnezzar as providing food and shelter to the wild animals and the birds, and indeed to "every creature"; the Babylonian Empire provided the stable society that allowed agriculture and trade to flourish, that built cities, that maintained law and order; everyone in the empire was dependent on the empire for the necessities of life; Nebuchadnezzar had the power of life and death over everyone in his empire. All of this is true. But what Nebuchadnezzar failed to realize was that all of this power and wealth, everything he had, had been given to him by God. It was God who had given him his extraordinary abilities, God who had given him success, God who had arranged the circumstances that had allowed him to conquer the world. And it was God who could take it all away in a moment.

Nebuchadnezzar's second problem, according to Daniel, was what he was doing with all the power that had been given to him. Nebuchadnezzar did not realize that with his power came responsibility. Since God had placed him in power, Nebuchadnezzar had an obligation to rule in accordance with God's wishes. This is where the rubber meets the road. It is one thing to acknowledge that God is "the Lord of kings" in theory and quite another to actually take orders from that Lord, to let God dictate government policy. In particular, Daniel told Nebuchadnezzar he had a responsibility to "do what is right" and "be kind to the oppressed" (4:27). In other words, Nebuchadnezzar, as head of the government, had a responsibility to provide justice and mercy, to punish the wicked and help people in trouble. This Nebuchadnezzar was apparently not doing, or Daniel would not have told him to change. Daniel, after all, was a chief administrator in Nebuchadnezzar's empire, and he knew what was going on. As a start, Nebuchadnezzar could have spent less money on his statues and palaces and more on meeting the needs of his subjects. Nebuchadnezzar made a revealing statement in 4:30. He described Babylon as his "royal residence" built "for the glory of my majesty." In other words, he considered the empire his personal property whose purpose was his own pleasure and pride. But God saw things differently. God saw Nebuchadnezzar's empire as Nebuchadnezzar's responsibility, as a vehicle that was to be used to bring justice and prosperity to the earth. This would take all the fun out of it, of course, making the emperorship a job rather than a privilege. In other words, God through Daniel was demanding that Nebuchadnezzar obey the principles that God had revealed to the people of Israel through the Old Testament law, that he do his best to make Babylon a just and ideal society, that he model his empire on the principles of the Kingdom of God. On the surface, the idea seems preposterous. Nebuchadnezzar had destroyed the nation of Israel, so why should he now adopt Jewish customs? The reason is that those customs did not belong to the Jewish people but were laws handed down by the God who was the Lord of the whole earth, Yahweh, the Creator of heaven and earth. Focused on his own empire, Nebuchadnezzar had forgotten the vision of the coming Kingdom of God that would replace Nebuchadnezzar's empire (chapter 2). That Kingdom of God would one day rise from humble beginnings to be the great tree that would provide food and shelter to the whole world (Matthew 13:31-32, Mark 4:30-32, Luke 13:18-19). In essence, God was demanding that Nebuchadnezzar stop building his own empire and become a servant of the Kingdom of God. It was an absolutely revolutionary thought, in every sense of the words. And yet that is what happened.

God's Purpose

Let us step back and ask a fundamental question. Why did Nebuchadnezzar have a dream about a tree that was chopped down? It wasn't just an accident, a confused product of a human brain as most dreams are. No, this dream was a vision, a revelation sent directly by God to Nebuchadnezzar. But why? To demonstrate God's knowledge of the future? To show Daniel's ability to interpret dreams? The dream is intricately connected to what happened afterward. Nebuchadnezzar had a dream about losing his kingdom, and then he lost his kingdom. Both of these events were arranged and controlled directly by God. Why? In the first place, God was revealing Himself directly to Nebuchadnezzar. God was proving to Nebuchadnezzar that He was indeed the God who controlled everything, including appointing and removing kings, that He was the God who knew the future because He controlled the future.

Now you must understand how revolutionary a change that was in order to understand why Nebuchadnezzar had such trouble understanding it. The gods that Nebuchadnezzar had worshiped all his life did not know everything. Their knowledge was limited. Further, they had not created the world, and they certainly didn't control it. Moreover, instead of there being one God, there were many gods, they often fought among themselves, and none of them had power to overcome all the others.

So, it was a revolutionary change for Nebuchadnezzar to grasp that there is only one, all-knowing, all-powerful God. But further we can ask why the dream came at that particular time, when Nebuchadnezzar had conquered Jerusalem and Daniel the Jew was present to interpret the dream. Why didn't God reveal Himself to Nebuchadnezzar so clearly in his dream that Nebuchadnezzar did not need Daniel there to interpret it? The answer is that God wanted to reveal Himself in such a way that the revelation would be connected to all the other things that God had revealed about Himself throughout history. Daniel was there to interpret the dream in order to show that this great God who was revealing Himself to Nebuchadnezzar was the God of the Jews, the God who had revealed Himself to and through God's people, Israel. That was a very detailed revelation and included the Old Testament law. This God of the Jews was not just the all-knowing, all-powerful Creator. He was also the God of justice and mercy and love and truth. This is what Daniel was teaching Nebuchadnezzar when he advised him to renounce his sins and wickedness, do what is right and be kind to the oppressed (4:27). Again we must understand how revolutionary this thought was to Nebuchadnezzar. The gods he had worshiped all his life were cruel and dishonest. In contrast, the true God is holy, demands that human beings be holy and judges human beings when they are not. It is no wonder that Nebuchadnezzar was not a just and merciful king because the gods he worshiped were not just and merciful. In sending His revelation, the dream and Daniel's interpretation, God was demanding that Nebuchadnezzar change his ideas and his way of living. Both changes would be revolutionary.

There is another aspect to this revelation. Remember that the Babylonians were convinced that "the gods...do not live among humans" (2:11). The Babylonian understanding of the gods was that they were remote, they didn't always pay attention to what was happening among human beings and they didn't particularly care what happened to human beings. Again the contrast to the God of the Bible is remarkable. Imagine a God who would arrange history so that Nebuchadnezzar would become king, expand his empire, conquer the Jews and make Daniel his advisor, a God who would send Nebuchadnezzar two dreams, not to mention the experience of the fiery furnace, and do all this precisely in order to reveal Himself to Nebuchadnezzar and change his life. This is a God who cares about human beings and will personally intervene in history for the sake of an individual human being, a God who knew and loved Nebuchadnezzar.

The revelation came to Nebuchadnezzar not just so he would know things about God. The revelation came because God loved Nebuchadnezzar and wanted to have a personal relationship with him and save him from his sins. Why would God care about a pagan king? Because Nebuchadnezzar, like all human beings, was a child of God. The revelation came not just so that Nebuchadnezzar would know but so that he would change.

A final note on the nature of prophecy. Why did God's intervention come in two parts, the dream and then the king's loss of his kingdom? Why didn't God just humble Nebuchadnezzar by deposing him? Why bother to send the dream first? There are two answers. One is that the dream came first so that Nebuchadnezzar would know without a doubt that it was God who had deposed him. The second is that if Nebuchadnezzar had paid attention to the dream, he need not have been deposed at all. We think of prophecy as God predicting the future, a future that cannot be changed because God is all-powerful and in control. It is true that God is all-powerful and in control, but that is not how God sees prophecy. The dream did not come to Nebuchadnezzar so God could say afterward, "I told you so." God sends prophecy as a warning and a promise. God sent the dream to tell Nebuchadnezzar to change his thinking and his life. It was a call to Nebuchadnezzar to repent and commit himself to the God who had been revealing Himself to Nebuchadnezzar in miraculous ways over the course of the past several years. With the experiences that Nebuchadnezzar had had, the dream should have been enough. But some people only learn things the hard way, by experience. When Nebuchadnezzar continued in his arrogance for another whole year (4:29-30), God followed through on His warning and deposed Nebuchadnezzar. Yahweh is the God who loves us so much that He keeps trying.

The Fulfillment of God's Purpose

The book of Daniel does not offer many details about what happened to Nebuchadnezzar. At least three things happened. First, Nebuchadnezzar lost his kingship. He was "driven away from people" (4:33)—he did not go of his own free will. We might assume there was a coup or a power struggle, which might have been reversed, for it was his advisors and nobles who later restored him to the throne (4:36). Second, Nebuchadnezzar seems to have suffered some kind of mental breakdown, since his "sanity" (Aramaic *manda*, which is variously translated as "wisdom," "intelligence," "knowledge," "reason" and "understanding") was later restored. Third, Nebuchadnezzar went out and lived like an animal. He ate "grass" (4:33, perhaps meaning any wild plants), he had no shelter from rain and dew, his hair grew long and matted until it looked like feathers, and his nails were allowed to grow long like claws. In other words, he did no personal grooming. This lifestyle was obviously related to Nebuchadnezzar's insanity; verse 16 says that his human mind would be replaced by the mind of an animal. It is ironic that in his dream, Nebuchadnezzar had seen himself as a great tree and his people as birds and animals, and now he himself was reduced to the status of an animal. He went from the top to the bottom in a moment. It is not clear which of the three events came first. Was he deposed because he had gone insane? Or did he go insane because he had been deprived of his kingdom? It is ironic that the man who was obeyed by millions, the man who had insisted that everyone in his vast empire worship him, was now suddenly alone. There is no record of anyone trying to find him or help him. It was as if everyone had forgotten him. Fame can disappear that quickly. There is no mention of even Daniel trying to help him, although Daniel might have had his own problems; if there was a coup, his own position and life might have been in danger. In any case, Daniel would know better than to interfere with the judgment and discipline of God.

How long this situation lasted, we are not sure. The "seven times" mentioned in verses 16, 23 and 32 are traditionally interpreted as seven years. However, the problem might have lasted seven months or seven weeks. Alternatively, "seven" is the number for heaven and the sabbath, and so the number might simply mean that Nebuchadnezzar was being forced to take a rest and be renewed. Or the number might simply be reinforcing the idea that it was God who was doing this to Nebuchadnezzar.

The sequence of Nebuchadnezzar's restoration is much clearer. The first thing that happened is that Nebuchadnezzar "raised (his) eyes toward heaven" (4:34). This is in keeping with the prophecy that Nebuchadnezzar would not be restored until he acknowledged that Heaven rules (4:26 and 4:17,25,32). Once Nebuchadnezzar had acknowledged God's supremacy, his sanity was restored (4:34), and so was his kingdom (4:36). There is an important lesson here—spiritual salvation precedes mental restoration and physical and circumstantial restoration.

Was this change in Nebuchadnezzar real and permanent? After all, he seems to have acknowledged the true God in chapters 2 and 3 without fundamentally changing his outlook. The evidence in Daniel 4 suggests that Nebuchadnezzar finally got it, that what we have witnessed here was a real conversion and that Nebuchadnezzar had become committed to following the one true God. Key evidence is that he wrote this proclamation praising the Most High God, publicly proclaiming his faith to the world. There is a qualitative difference between this proclamation and the one he issued in chapter 3. In chapter 3, Nebuchadnezzar was still acting from a position of power, giving orders as to what other people should do (3:29). Here in chapter 4, his approach was quite different. Instead of lording it over other people, he was humbly admitting that God was lord over him. Second, while in chapters 2 and 3 Nebuchadnezzar had praised the power of God, here he also acknowledged the justice and holiness of God (4:37)—he was learning to know the nature of God. Third, in chapter 2, Nebuchadnezzar praised Daniel's God (2:47). In chapter 3, he praised "the God of Shadrach, Meshach and Abednego" (3:28-29). But here in chapter 4, he praised "the Most High" (4:34) and "the King of heaven" (4:37). The God of Daniel, Hananiah, Mishael and Azariah was now also the God of Nebuchadnezzar. Nebuchadnezzar had apparently committed his life to serving the one true God. Many years later, in chapter 5, Daniel still spoke highly of Nebuchadnezzar's submission to God, in contrast to the arrogance of Nebuchadnezzar's descendant Belshazzar (5:18-22).

The logical conclusion is that Nebuchadnezzar will be in heaven with all other true worshipers of God. Sadly, the same can probably not be said of Zedekiah, the last king of Judah. Scripture records that Zedekiah "did evil in the eyes of the LORD his God and did not humble himself before Jeremiah the prophet, who spoke the word of the LORD...He became stiff-necked and hardened his heart and would not turn to the LORD, the God of Israel" (2 Chronicles 36:12-13, 2 Kings 24:19). Twice in his final days, Zedekiah consulted Jeremiah the prophet, and twice Jeremiah advised him to surrender to the Babylonians and save his life and the lives of his people (Jeremiah 37:16-21, 38:14-28). But Zedekiah refused, unwilling to trust his life to God. We do not know what Zedekiah might have done in his final days, blind, defeated and in prison, but unless he repented then, he will not be with Nebuchadnezzar in heaven. Both kings were given direct revelation from God over a number of years, both had a major prophet of Yahweh to advise them, both were deposed from their thrones, but only Nebuchadnezzar seems to have responded by placing his faith in God.

An interesting sidelight is that Zedekiah had placed Jeremiah in prison, but Nebuchadnezzar, when he destroyed Jerusalem, sent specific orders that Jeremiah was to be released and protected (Jeremiah 39:11-14). This was possibly due to the intervention of Daniel, but it also shows Nebuchadnezzar's new respect for the God of Israel and

Yahweh's prophets. In fact, when Nebuchadnezzar's army general, Nebuzaradan, released Jeremiah, Nebuzaradan stated very clearly that it was Israel's God, Yahweh, who had caused Israel's defeat as a result of Israel's unfaithfulness to Yahweh. And then he gave Jeremiah provisions and a present (Jeremiah 40:1-6).

Collateral Conversions

In this chapter, God intervened to save Nebuchadnezzar, to turn his life around. But God can do many things at once. In intervening to teach and save Nebuchadnezzar, God was intervening to teach and save other human beings as well. What God had done for Nebuchadnezzar would be a revelation to everyone in the Babylonian Empire and many people outside it—not to mention the billions of people who have since read about it in the Bible. His proclamation has reached its intended audience, the whole world. What happens to an emperor gets noticed.

We do not know how widely Nebuchadnezzar's proclamation was distributed or what effect it had. We can be sure that it probably received more attention than the proclamation of a king of Judah might have received. As mentioned above, we know that Nebuchadnezzar's army general, Nebuzaradan, now understood who Yahweh was and what He was doing. We know that the wisdom of Daniel might have been well known in Tyre, the great city state in what is now Lebanon (Ezekiel 28:3, although this reference might refer to another man named Daniel). We also know that some non-Jews in the Persian Empire (which succeeded the Babylonian Empire) gave freewill offerings to the Jews for the rebuilding of Yahweh's temple (Ezra 1:1-6, 6:1-16) and that by the time of Jesus, Judaism had attracted proselytes, converts, from a wide variety of nations (Acts 2:5-11).

We don't know what impact Nebuchadnezzar's conversion had on his own family. When he died in 562 BC, he was succeeded by his son Amel-Marduk (or Evil-Merodach, which means "The man is Marduk"—Marduk was another of the Babylonian gods). Interestingly, Amel-Marduk released Jehoiachin, the second last king of Judah, from prison, where he had been ever since 597 BC. Was this due to Daniel's influence, or was it a sign of Amel-Marduk's respect for Judah's God? Even later, in 539 BC, the "queen" (we will discuss later who she might have been) reminded the new king, Belshazzar, about Daniel and what Nebuchadnezzar had learned from him. We do not know if other members of Nebuchadnezzar's family also became followers of the Most High God.

The Wise Men

However, we do have a hint about the impact the presence of Daniel and his friends seems to have had on one group of people. The silent witnesses to everything that happened in chapter 4 were the "magicians, enchanters, astrologers and diviners" of Babylon (4:7). These people were to some extent considered colleagues of Daniel, Hananiah, Mishael and Azariah. Chapter 4 represents the second time that they had seen Daniel's God interpret a royal dream that they could not interpret. After their first failure in chapter 2, some of them responded with jealousy, trying to have Hananiah, Mishael and Azariah thrown into the furnace in chapter 3. That resulted in them again seeing the power of the God of the Jews. After their second failure to interpret a royal dream, there is no record of them again trying to seek revenge.

But what was their attitude? Did some of them have a hand in the coup that temporarily deposed Nebuchadnezzar? We don't know.

But we do know something. Matthew 2:1-12, in the New Testament part of the Bible, tells the familiar story of the "wise men" coming to worship the baby Jesus. The story forms part of Christmas celebrations every year all over the world. But do we ever think about the significance of the story? Who were these men, and why did they come? The Christmas carol calls them kings and focuses on the expensive presents they brought. But the Bible does not call them kings. It calls them "wise men" or "magi," from which we derive our word "magician." They studied the stars and were probably astrologers, people who thought they could interpret and predict world events by studying the movements of the stars. And they came from "the east" to Palestine to worship Jesus. The obvious conclusion is that they were some of the successors of the "magicians, enchanters, astrologers and diviners" (Daniel 4:7), the "wise men" who had advised the king of Babylon (Daniel 4:6). These were the same people as the "magicians, enchanters, sorcerers and astrologers" in Daniel 2:2, who were called simply "astrologers" throughout the rest of chapter 2 and in chapter 3. Their tradition of seeking wisdom through astrology had seemingly survived from the time of Nebuchadnezzar through the fall of Babylon until the birth of Jesus Christ almost 600 years later.

So, we know who these men were, but why would they come to worship the one who was "born king of the Jews" (Matthew 2:2)? Judah was not even an independent nation then. One might undertake a journey of several months to see the future Roman emperor perhaps, but why the king of an obscure people like the Jews? And why bring expensive presents? These men weren't Jewish, so why would a Jewish king matter to them? They obviously had some knowledge that convinced them that the birth of Jesus was important to them. What could it be? They didn't know the Old Testament prophecy of Micah (5:2-4, quoted in Matthew 2:6) that had foretold that Jesus would be born in Bethlehem or they wouldn't have had to stop in Jerusalem to ask for directions (Matthew 2:2). But their predecessors had certainly been well acquainted with Daniel, and, unlike the rest of the Old Testament, the book of Daniel was mostly written in Aramaic, a language they could understand. This might be one of the reasons why the book of Daniel was written in Aramaic to begin with. It is entirely possible that the wise men of Babylon still had in their possession a copy of this book or at the very least knew of its contents. But that still does not explain why they were convinced the birth of Jesus mattered to them. Yet the answer is obvious. Daniel chapter 2 contained the prophecy of the four empires that were to be replaced by the Kingdom of God that would take over government of the entire world. Six hundred years later, the descendants of the wise men of Babylon would have been able to see that the prophecy had been absolutely correct in predicting the fate of the Babylonian, Persian, Greek and Roman Empires. The prophecy of Daniel 2 was supplemented by the more detailed prophecy of the later chapters of Daniel, and it is possible the later wise men had a copy of those as well, although they weren't written in Aramaic. Still, Daniel 2 would have been sufficient to convince the wise men that the prophecy was nearing the time of its fulfillment and that the Kingdom of God would soon be established. Why would it matter to them? Because the wise men of Babylon had been eyewitnesses of the events that had taken place during the time of Daniel. They had seen that the God of the Jews had interpreted dreams that they couldn't interpret, had rescued Hananiah, Mishael and Azariah from the furnace and had humbled Emperor Nebuchadnezzar. It is possible that at least some of them had become convinced that Yahweh, the God of the Jews, was the only true God. It is possible that some of them had become followers of the Most High God, just as Nebuchadnezzar had. If so, then it is possible that some of their successors also believed in the true God and were ready to become part of the Kingdom of God that was initiated by the birth of Jesus Christ. They might not have understood perfectly. They still seem to have been practicing some aspects of astrology. But no other reason would explain why they would travel all that distance and bring such expensive gifts. Although it is not widely known now, after the death and resurrection of Jesus, the early Christian church expanded quite quickly into the area that had once been the center of the Babylonian Empire. Was the way prepared by Daniel and the well-known conversion of Nebuchadnezzar?

The God of History

Throughout history, God has called a wide variety of people to follow Him. We think that in the Old Testament God worked only with His chosen people, the Israelites, and later with the last surviving tribe of the Israelites, the Jews. But it is not true. Many of the Israelites who had grown up knowing about God were unfaithful to Him, going off after other gods. In contrast, many pagan people around Israel became followers of the true God. Among them were the "many other people" who joined Israel's exodus out of Egypt (Exodus 12:38); Rahab the prostitute (Joshua 2, 6:22-23); Caleb, one of only two adults who had crossed through the Red Sea who was considered worthy to be allowed into the Promised Land (Numbers 32:12); Ruth, the ancestor of David (Ruth); and the hundreds of Kerethites, Pelethites and Gittites (Philistines) who had begun following David when he was hiding out in Gath and who remained faithful to him through Absalom's rebellion (2 Samuel 15:16-22).

The history of the Christian church is similar. A tiny Jewish Christian church evangelized the Roman Empire. When European barbarians invaded the Roman Empire, the Christians converted the Europeans. When Vikings from even farther north invaded Europe, the Christians converted the Vikings.

Despite the repeated evidence of history, we are somehow convinced that people don't change, that only people from a Christian background become Christians. The fact is that God gives His Kingdom to whomever He wishes. The fact is that God repeatedly calls the most unlikely people to follow Him—and they do!

Dare to Be a Daniel

As a young man, Daniel was carried off into exile in a foreign country and compelled to serve in the court of a pagan king. A crowd of pagan magicians and powerful world leaders attempted to force Daniel to adopt their way of life.

But in the end it was the rulers and magicians who changed, becoming followers of the Most High God. While much more powerful than Daniel, they were no match for the God Daniel believed in. We, too, are surrounded by pagan forces that are attempting to squeeze us into their mold. Are we changing? Or are the pagans around us changing? *Can* the pagans around us change?

Christians often talk about "witnessing." It sounds like an onerous and complicated duty. But "witnessing" is simply doing what witnesses do in court, telling what we have seen and heard. In this case, we are to tell people what we have seen and heard about the one true God.

As Christians, we have come to know the one true God who is all-powerful but also holy, just but also loving and forgiving, having sent His Son Jesus to die for our sins. We know the God who cares about us and has come to live in our hearts, the God who has invited us to come into His eternal Kingdom. This God has given us clear orders: "All authority in heaven and on earth has been given to me. Therefore go and make disciples of all nations, baptizing them in the name of the Father and of the Son and of the Holy Spirit, and teaching them to obey everything I have commanded you. And surely I am with you always, to the very end of the age" (Matthew 28:18-20) and "You will receive power when the Holy Spirit comes on you; and you will be my witnesses in Jerusalem, and in all Judea and Samaria, and to the ends of the earth" (Acts 1:8).

Are we obeying this command? Are people around us coming to believe in God as we do? This chapter raises several issues or questions concerning how we go about witnessing to the reality of the Most High God.

First, we should not underestimate what we are asking people to do. We are asking them to completely change their orientation. God is calling for a revolution, a complete change in loyalty and purpose. God is demanding that people change their primary loyalty from their own kingdoms to God's Kingdom. Before we witness, we should examine ourselves.

Are we preoccupied with building our own empires instead of focusing on building God's Kingdom? If we are focused on our own kingdoms, we might be selfish enough to ask whether we want to risk our jobs or our reputations or even our lives by witnessing to the reality of the Most High God. But if we are focused on God's Kingdom in whatever we do, a primary focus will be on inviting the pagans around us to join us in worshiping the one true God, regardless of the consequences.

Second, it is important to note that surprising bit of information that was mentioned earlier. Daniel seems to have come to the point where he cared deeply about what happened to the pagan king who had enslaved him. Daniel had come to love Nebuchadnezzar and see Nebuchadnezzar as his friend. If our witnessing efforts are not as successful as Daniel's were, perhaps the problem is that we don't love as Daniel did. Do we really care what happens to the pagan people around us? Do we see them as lost people who need our help, people whom God loves and whom He sent His Son Jesus to save? Or are we blinded into seeing them only as enemies?

The third question concerns a problem that Daniel had and that we may share—fear. Daniel was "greatly perplexed" and "terrified" and had to be encouraged to speak by Nebuchadnezzar (4:19). Daniel's task was to tell King Nebuchadnezzar that God was going to depose him from being king. The words amounted to treason. Can you imagine the courage it took to tell the most powerful emperor in the world that he was doing the wrong things (giving specific details—4:27) and that if he didn't change, God would punish him? Like Daniel, we are often afraid to give bad news. No one likes to hear about judgment. In North America, surveys tell us that ninety percent of Americans believe there is a heaven—and are convinced they are going to go there! No one wants to hear that he or she is a sinner facing the judgment of Almighty God. People don't want to hear that adultery or abortion or homosexual practice or greed or pride or gossip is sinful. But if there is no bad news, there is no good news either. We can't preach salvation to people who don't know they are lost. At the beginning of the church, the apostle Peter accused the people in Jerusalem of crucifying the Son of God (Acts 2:36). Terrified, they asked, "What shall we do?" (Acts 2:37) Peter responded, "Repent and be baptized, every one of you, in the name of Jesus Christ for the forgiveness of your sins. And you will receive the gift of the Holy Spirit. The promise is for you and your children and for all who are far off—for all whom the Lord our God will call" (Acts 2:38-39). The Most High God did not send Daniel to the court of Nebuchadnezzar, trouble Nebuchadnezzar with dreams and depose Nebuchadnezzar from his throne in order to punish this pagan emperor. God did it in order to turn Nebuchadnezzar around, to rescue him from his own sinfulness. The Most High God did not send His Son Jesus into the world to condemn it but to save it (John 3:17). We need to tell people about the God of Heaven, who convicts us and saves us from sin. We need to tell people about the coming Kingdom of God and that it is only open to people who submit to the King.

Perhaps the most profound question this chapter raises is the fourth and last one. I suspect that the main reason why so many of us often do not tell people about the Most High God is that we don't think it will do any good. Seeing all of the negative trends in our society—from increasing sin to decreasing church attendance—we don't think there is anything we can do to reverse the trends. Recognizing that the pagans have won, we make the mistake of thinking that that victory is permanent and irreversible. We have become convinced that no one will listen. We have fallen into the error of thinking that it is all up to our own futile efforts and forgetting that the God of Heaven is still intervening in the lives of people to empower our witness and change the hearts of sinful human beings.

When I attended university in the 1970s, there were only a handful of committed Christians in my dorm of over 200 students. I offered a free Bible to anyone in the residence who would take one and made no secret of my faith in Jesus, but that made little impact. In my third year, two brothers, fervent Christians, moved into the dorm. And I mean fervent—they played hymns on their trumpets in the stairwell at 6:00 a.m. They urged us older Christians to start "an evangelistic worship service" in the dorm. We carefully explained to them that the students in the dorm were thoroughly paganized—they weren't interested and wouldn't come. However, these young men persisted, and we finally agreed to try it—and they inexplicably left the leadership to those of us who were doubtful about the whole enterprise to begin with. About thirty-five students showed up the first week. That evangelistic service ran on Sunday evenings for the next several years, it became well known all across campus, and the last meeting of every year featured testimonies of those who had come to faith in Jesus Christ through that evangelistic service that year.

In a pagan culture dominated by the forces of evil, it is very easy to give up on telling people about the God of Heaven and lapse into silence. Such thinking overlooks the power of God to intervene to change people's minds. If God can reach Nebuchadnezzar and the sorcerers of Babylon, He can reach anybody in our society. This is the third commitment that we need to make:

Knowing that God can convert pagans, I will witness.

Chapter 6
Love Your Enemies
Jeremiah 29:1-23

The Context

While Daniel and his friends were coping with being in exile, the Jews back in Jerusalem were also trying to understand what was happening and how they should respond to the new situation.

In the fourth year of Zedekiah, that is, about 593 BC, a dozen years after Nebuchadnezzar had first come to Jerusalem and sent Daniel and his friends into exile, and four years after Nebuchadnezzar had conquered Jerusalem a second time and sent more Jews into exile, the prophet Jeremiah made a pronouncement (Jeremiah 27:1, 28:1). By this time, Jeremiah had been a prophet for about twenty-five years. He had denounced the sinfulness of the Jewish nation, called for repentance and foretold that Babylon would invade Judah as punishment for Judah's sins. So far, his prophecies were coming true. Now, Jeremiah proclaimed another message he said had come from Yahweh, the God of Israel, the true God. It was not a very encouraging message. Jeremiah put on his shoulders a yoke such as was used by oxen to pull plows and carts. He then advised the people of Judah and the other nations around Judah to serve the Babylonians as oxen serve their masters. He promised that if they served the Babylonians, things would go well for them; but if they did not, the Babylonians would destroy them. In particular, he warned that the Babylonians would destroy Jerusalem and the temple of Yahweh; while the Babylonians had already taken many of the gold articles out of the temple, the Babylonians would now take the larger objects as well, such as two huge metal pillars and some other objects, which would have to be cut up in order to be transported. (All of this is related in Jeremiah 27.)

But there were other prophets speaking as well. One of them, Hananiah, took the yoke off Jeremiah's shoulders and broke it. He declared that within two years Yahweh would defeat the Babylonians and bring the temple articles and the exiles back from Babylon (Jeremiah 28:1-4,10-11). This was an encouraging prophecy and a very optimistic prophecy. But God's prophets had previously foretold Judah's deliverance through the unexpected collapse of the Assyrian Empire, and that had occurred only about fifteen years earlier when Babylon had overthrown Assyria.

If you were in Jerusalem, whom would you have believed? If you had been in exile with Daniel and his friends, whom would you have believed? (Reports of the prophecies were sent to the exiles in Babylon.) It is not always easy to know what God is doing, and Satan always tries to confuse God's message with conflicting messages of his own.

The best test of whether a prophet had been sent by the true God was if the prophet's words came true: "You may say to yourselves, 'How can we know when a message has not been spoken by the LORD?' If what a prophet declares in the name of the LORD does not take place or come true, that is a message the LORD has not spoken" (Deuteronomy 18:21-22). The problem was that in this case the people had to make decisions and choices, and those choices depended on what they thought God was doing. They had to know whether to rebel against Babylon or not. One clue was that Hananiah had prophesied the destruction of Babylon within two years. Babylon had first conquered Jerusalem about 605 BC, and Hananiah spoke about 593 BC. So, when Babylon was not destroyed by 591 BC, the people should have known that Hananiah's prophecy was wrong and Jeremiah's prophecy was right. Moreover, Jeremiah received another prophecy, that God would strike Hananiah dead within a year as punishment for his false prophecy (Jeremiah 28:12-17). He died within two months. If they had known of this prophecy, the Jews might have concluded that Hananiah was wrong. But it seems that this prophecy was given to Hananiah alone, to give him an opportunity to repent before he died. Hananiah's death alone should have given the Jews pause. But it seems that the majority of Jews believed Hananiah (Jeremiah 28:15).

Jeremiah then sent a letter (Jeremiah 29:1-23) to the exiles in Babylon (entrusting it to some royal envoys) in order to share with the exiles the prophecies God had given him.

The Content

Letters from home are often very welcome. It is likely that Jeremiah's letter to the exiles in Babylon was not. Those taken into exile with Daniel in 605 BC were primarily young. The same is likely true of those taken into exile after Jehoiachin's rebellion in 597 BC. According to 2 Kings 24:13-16, they were composed of three groups—about 7,000 soldiers (who would either be forced into the Babylonian army or at least kept neutral in Babylon), 1,000 craftsmen and artisans (who would be set to work building Babylon and Nebuchadnezzar's palaces) and perhaps 2,000 members of the upper class, members of the royal family and the nobility. We do not know if those numbers include the wives and children of the soldiers and artisans or if their families were taken in addition. Jeremiah 52:28-30 might suggest that the 10,000 included families. Those verses do not say how many went into exile with Daniel in 605 BC but state that 3,023 Jews went into exile in Nebuchadnezzar's seventh year, which would have been when Jehoiachin's rebellion was crushed in 597 BC, a number considerably smaller than the 10,000 figure in Kings. Perhaps Jeremiah counted only heads of families or, since the number is very precise, only those recorded on some kind of list, whose names were known (see Ezra 2:62).

Whatever their number, all of these exiles had arrived in a foreign land, not knowing what would happen to them and hoping that they would someday be able to go home again. Jeremiah's message would have dashed those hopes. It would have come as very unwelcome news. Jeremiah was saying that the exile would last seventy years. Seventy years is a lifetime, more than a lifetime if you have already lived for a few years. The exiles' grandchildren might see the Promised Land, but they would not. They would die in exile.

One can readily see how the exiles might misunderstand Jeremiah's message. They could understand Jeremiah to be saying that there was no hope, that they might as well give up because there was nothing they could do, that there was no point in going on. But that is not what Jeremiah was saying. Jeremiah told the exiles that there were four things that they could—and should—be doing. It is important for us to understand that these were not suggestions or good advice. They were commands from God (Jeremiah 29:4).

First, Jeremiah told the exiles to "build houses and settle down; plant gardens and eat what they produce" (Jeremiah 29:5). In other words, they were to work, earn a living, provide for their own basic physical needs. God had put them there, and God wanted them alive for some reason. But they weren't just to eat and stay alive. They were to work for what they needed to stay alive, be productive. It would not be easy. It would be hard, starting over in a foreign land. But the commands of God are not about what is easy but about what is right.

Second, Jeremiah told the exiles to "marry and have sons and daughters; find wives for your sons and give your daughters in marriage, so that they too may have sons and daughters. Increase in number there; do not decrease" (Jeremiah 29:6). This is, in essence, a repetition of the very first command that God gave to human beings: "Be fruitful and increase in number; fill the earth and subdue it" (Genesis 1:28).

In our days of "population explosion," when we have to a large extent "filled the earth," we do not see much urgency in such a command. After all, the human sex drive is ever present and powerful, and producing babies is what people do. But the command to the Jewish exiles through Jeremiah was not to have sex or produce babies. It was to get married and raise families. After all, in the past as in the present, babies can be disposed of through abortion or neglect—it was quite common in the past to put babies out into the woods and leave them to die. Having sex can be a purely selfish act. But raising a family is an act of extreme unselfishness, demanding a lifetime of commitment and hard work. It is true—and more so in the past than the present—that children can help their parents in their old age. But having children is not primarily like earning one's own living. For the Jewish exiles, as it is for people in most times and places, having children was not primarily for their benefit but for the benefit of their children and grandchildren.

What was the primary purpose of raising families in this case? It was so that when the people of God were allowed to go home in seventy years' time, there would be some children of God alive to do it. And more than that, the purpose was so that when it came time for the people of God to return home, there would be people *willing* to go. Inherent in this raising of families would be the raising of *Jewish* families, people who understood the nature and purposes of God, people who were committed to following God's ways. It was so that there would be people who would be willing to leave the settled existence in Babylon that their parents had carved out for them, leave the only life they had ever known, in order to "return" to a land they had never seen and start all over from scratch. It would take deeply committed people to rebuild a viable nation in a land devastated by war and neglect. The purpose of this second command was the survival of the people of God on earth, the building of the Kingdom of God.

Like Abraham and Zechariah, they were to have children, not for their own benefit, but for the sake of God's purposes, that all the peoples of the earth would be blessed (Genesis 12:1-3, Luke 1:11-17). The people fulfilling this command would never see the fruit of it, never see the restored Kingdom of God in the Promised Land; only their grandchildren would. Fulfilling this command would be an act of obedience, unselfishness, faith and hope.

Third—and to the Jewish exiles this would have been the most incomprehensible part of the message—they were told to "seek the peace and prosperity of the city to which I have carried you into exile. Pray to the LORD for it, because if it prospers, you too will prosper" (Jeremiah 29:7). God was telling the Jewish exiles to help the Babylonians, the evil pagan empire that had destroyed their nation, carried them into exile and slaughtered their friends and families. They weren't just to submit to Babylon; they were to work to make Babylon richer and healthier and more stable. And they were to pray that God would bless Babylon.

For Daniel and his three friends, this would mean working hard and creatively in the Babylonian civil service. Like Joseph earlier in Egypt (Genesis 39-50), they were to be loyal servants of the foreign tyrant who had enslaved them. We don't naturally love our oppressors. The movie *Bridge on the River Kwai* tells the story of Allied prisoners of war during World War Two who were mistreated horribly and required to build a bridge for their cruel Japanese captors. The urge to build the bridge but secretly sabotage it by planting bombs within it that would destroy it was overwhelming. Daniel and his friends must have been tempted to do the same thing, to appear to work for the Babylonian Empire while undermining it from within. But this is exactly what God was telling them not to do. They were to wholeheartedly serve King Nebuchadnezzar. Sometimes that would involve challenging his authority to show him the truth about the one true God. Sometimes it would involve challenging his policies by telling him to treat his people fairly (Daniel 4:27). But mostly it would involve working diligently every day to make the Babylonian government work efficiently. Daniel and his friends did this. "Daniel so distinguished himself among the administrators...by his exceptional qualities" (Daniel 6:3) that he was frequently promoted. When his enemies tried to find something they could accuse him of, "they could find no corruption in him because he was trustworthy and neither corrupt nor negligent" (Daniel 6:4). What Daniel and his friends did, all of the exiles were commanded to do. What God was commanding them to do was to love their enemies wholeheartedly and unconditionally.

Praying for Babylon would be just as difficult. The temptation would be to pray for the peace of Jerusalem and to pray that God would curse Babylon and the other enemies of God—as some of the Psalms seem to do. But God loved Babylon, and the Jewish exiles were to encourage God to continue to love Babylon.

Now, there was an immediate promise that went along with this command: "If it prospers, you too will prosper" (Jeremiah 29:7). This need not be considered an extraordinary or miraculous consequence. It is just common sense. If believers live in a prosperous society, they will likely be prosperous. If they live in a society that is characterized by law and order, they will be relatively safe. Babylon was a wealthy and ordered society, and the Jewish exiles in general did very well. There is perhaps a parallel with the earlier Bible story of Joseph being taken as a slave to Egypt. He eventually rose to be the chief administrator in that land. By working hard for the Egyptian Empire, he saved that country from the effects of a severe famine, and in so doing also saved his own family, who were the people of God (Genesis 37-50).

Fourth, Jeremiah told the exiles, "Do not let the prophets and diviners among you deceive you. Do not listen to the dreams you encourage them to have" (Jeremiah 29:8). The fourth duty of the exiles was to not listen to false prophets. Not only were there false prophets such as Hananiah in Jerusalem. There were also false prophets among the exiles.

We know the names of three of them: Ahab son of Kolaiah, Zedekiah son of Maaseiah (Jeremiah 29:21) and Shemaiah the Nehelamite (Jeremiah 29:31). These men were claiming to speak in the name of Yahweh (Jeremiah 29:9,21,23,31). They were apparently saying that there was no point in the exiles getting settled in Babylon because they would soon be going home to Jerusalem. It is very clear that such a message would be far more welcome to the exiles than Jeremiah's message of a long captivity, the destruction of Jerusalem and the necessity to work hard for both the Kingdom of God and the Babylonian Empire. In fact, Jeremiah said that the exiles were encouraging these false prophecies (Jeremiah 29:8) and believing them (Jeremiah 29:31).

The problem was that these "prophecies" were "lies" (Jeremiah 29:9,21,23,31) and that they had not come from God. God declared in essence, "I have not sent them." This was a very serious matter because these self-declared prophets were breaking the Third Commandment: "You shall not misuse the name of the LORD your God" (Exodus 20:7). Their actions caused people to do the opposite of what God was commanding. Thus they were preaching "rebellion" against the true God (Jeremiah 29:32). The Third Commandment contains a warning of punishment: "The LORD will not hold anyone guiltless who misuses his name" (Exodus 20:7). Through Jeremiah, God pronounced His punishment on the false prophets. Ahab and Zedekiah would be burned to death by King Nebuchadnezzar (Jeremiah 29:21-22), and Shemaiah and all his family would also die in exile (Jeremiah 29:32). We should not be lulled into complacency by the miraculous deliverance of Hananiah, Mishael and Azariah from Nebuchadnezzar's furnace. Nebuchadnezzar was a cruel king who used capital punishment freely. The false prophets were among those who died in his furnaces.

But all this comes back to the question of how the exiles were supposed to know which of the competing prophets were speaking true messages from Yahweh and which were not. One solution to this dilemma was to know God very well.

Those who knew the true God would know that He is a moral God who insists on moral actions from His followers. The false prophets Ahab and Zedekiah had apparently committed adultery and had not seen anything wrong with it (Jeremiah 29:23). Their understanding of God was flawed. Moreover, they were promising God's forgiveness, blessing and restoration without any mention of repentance. On the other hand, God, speaking through Jeremiah, promised restoration only "when you seek me with all your heart" (Jeremiah 29:13).

Now here is an important question: Did the Jewish exiles do as they were told? Did they obey God's commands through Jeremiah? We know that Daniel read and heeded Jeremiah's message (Daniel 9:1ff). Certainly not all of the exiles did, and there are indications that the exiles at first preferred the pleasant prophecies of the false prophets. But Jeremiah was eventually proved right when Jerusalem was destroyed, and a significant number of the exiles seem to have obeyed Jeremiah's message.

The Promise

Jeremiah's message contained more than a list of commands. It also contained God's firm promise: "When seventy years are completed for Babylon, I will come to you and fulfill my good promise to bring you back to this place...back from captivity. I will gather you from all the nations and places where I have banished you...and will bring you back to the place from which I carried you into exile" (Jeremiah 29:10-14).

We know that this promise was fulfilled. In 539 BC, the Babylonian Empire was defeated by the Medes and Persians. The Persian emperor, Cyrus, reversed the Babylonian policy of transferring conquered peoples from their homelands. Specifically, he decreed that the Jews were to return to Palestine, rebuild Jerusalem and re-establish their nation (although still under the authority of the Persian Empire). He even gave the Jews the gold and other metal objects that

Nebuchadnezzar had taken from Yahweh's temple in Jerusalem. The Jews were to rebuild the temple and resume the worship of Yahweh. The Persian Empire even provided financial assistance for these tasks (Ezra 6:3-10, 7:12-24, Nehemiah 2:1-9).

Now here is where the Jews' obedience to God's commandments became important. When God was ready to restore the Jews to Palestine, were the Jews ready to go back? Had the exiles done as they were told? Had they grown in numbers and become prosperous in anticipation of the return? We don't know how many Jews had gone into exile with Daniel in 605 BC. About 10,000 went into exile after the crushing of Jehoiachin's rebellion in 597 BC (2 Kings 24:15-17). We do not know how many went into exile after Nebuchadnezzar destroyed Jerusalem in 587 BC. Jeremiah 52:28-30 says 832 people from Jerusalem went into exile in Nebuchadnezzar's eighteenth year, which would have been in 587 BC. In that case, many of the Jews must have been executed as traitors instead of being sent into exile (Jeremiah 39:1-10). Jeremiah 52:28-30 also states that a further 745 Jews were taken into exile in Nebuchadnezzar's twenty-third year. This was probably a further punishment after Gedaliah, the Jew the Babylonians had appointed as governor to administer Palestine after the destruction of Jerusalem, was assassinated (Jeremiah 40:7-41:15). In any case, the numbers listed in Jeremiah 52:28-30 seem unrealistically small but very precise, so it is possible they refer to only some of the exiles, those whose names were known. Whatever the precise number, we can guess that the number who went into exile might have been somewhere between 10,000 and 20,000.

How many returned? We know that about 50,000 Jews returned in the first wave in 538 BC. (Others returned later, although a significant number chose to stay in Babylon, where they were prospering.) Having gone into exile with nothing, the first wave of returning exiles brought with them 736 horses, 245 mules, 435 camels and 6,720 donkeys—and all the material wealth these beasts could carry (Ezra 2:64-67). They were also able to contribute what amounts to thousands of dollars in gold and silver to the rebuilding of the temple (Ezra 2:68-69). They were not wealthy, but they were far from the destitute refugees who had gone into exile. It appears that the Jewish exiles had obeyed God and grown in numbers and wealth. Obeying God had paid off in the long run.

As impressive as the return from Babylon to Jerusalem was, this was not all there was to God's promise—and not even the most important thing. Jeremiah's prophecy also contained this commandment and promise: "Then you will call upon me and come and pray to me, and I will listen to you. You will seek me and find me when you seek me with all your heart. I will be found by you" (Jeremiah 29:12-14). It was a promise of spiritual renewal, of a return to intimacy with God. It was a privilege for the Jews to return to the Promised Land given to their ancestors. But how much greater was the privilege of becoming reacquainted with the God who had created the universe!

Through Jeremiah, God promised, "I know the plans I have for you, plans to prosper you and not to harm you, plans to give you hope and a future" (Jeremiah 29:11). God was saying that all that was happening, including the destruction of Jerusalem and the exile in Babylon, was part of God's plan. It had not happened by accident. Moreover, it was part of God's plan for good. It was designed to help the Jews, not harm them. In fact, if the Jews in Jerusalem had surrendered to Babylon without a fight as Jeremiah had advised, hardly any of them would have suffered harm at all, and the nation would have grown and prospered even more than it did. And then the Jews, now refined by exile, would be sent back to Jerusalem, where they would rebuild the city and the temple.

But even that was not all of God's plan. God's plan was bigger than that. Why were the Jews to return? Not just to rebuild a city or a temple, but to prepare a place for Jesus to come to, to prepare a place for the coming of the great rock

(Daniel 2:34-35,44-45), the Kingdom of God that would replace all other kingdoms and fill the earth. The exile and return were designed to prepare the Jews for that role.

But God's plan was even bigger still. In God's plan, the exile was also designed to spread knowledge of the one true God throughout the Babylonian Empire and throughout the world. Through the conversion of Nebuchadnezzar, through some of God's other miraculous actions and simply through the scattering of the Jews through many nations, it did that. The exile was destined to prepare not just the Jews but also the whole world for the coming of the Messiah. When Jesus came, He was welcomed by the Babylonian magi and by representatives of many nations who had come to Jerusalem to worship the one true God (Acts 2:5-11). God's plan was bigger than any of the Jews could see, and it was a plan for good.

It is important to state that the Jews did not need to see the full extent of God's plan. All that was required of them was to be obedient and perform the tasks that God had assigned to them—to earn their living, build houses, raise families and seek the prosperity of the society around them. It is in such little ways that the Kingdom of God comes upon the earth.

How Do We Know Which Prophets Are Right Today?

When I was in university, I came across a small book by David Wilkerson called *The Vision*. In this book, Wilkerson presented a modern prophecy that God was going to pour out a terrible judgment on the world in general and the United States in particular. In response, George Otis wrote a book called *The Blueprint*, in which he declared that God loved the United States and in which he prophesied that a great spiritual revival would rescue the United States from the impending judgment. I remember my excitement when I recognized the same dilemma that had faced the people of God in the time of Jeremiah and Daniel: Which prophets should we believe? Which set of instructions should we follow? What should we do? In the half-century since those books were published, while both authors have been proven correct on some points, it has become clear that in their broad outline neither prophecy has been fulfilled.

Yet the dilemma remains for us. How do we "discern the times"? How do we know what God is doing? How can we know what we should be doing? The biblical test of waiting to see whether a prophecy will come true doesn't seem very helpful here. We need to know what to do now.

I did not know in the 1970s whether Wilkerson's or Otis's prophecy would come true. But I had begun studying the Bible, and I knew something about the God of the Bible. I knew that God is a God of love and redemption but also a God of judgment. I knew that those who take a light view of sin are wrong and that God does punish people and nations for sin. I knew that God loves us and freely wants to offer us salvation. I also knew that the blessing of God only comes with repentance. I didn't know whether Wilkerson or Otis would eventually be proven right. But I did know what God wanted. He wanted me and my society to repent and turn to Him. I didn't know what God was doing, but I knew very clearly what God wanted me to do. While it is easy to discern that North American society is falling away from God and becoming a pagan society, I do not know if North America as a whole will repent, and I do not know how many North Americans will individually repent. But I do know that repentance is necessary for God's blessing. And I do know that God's commands through Jeremiah to a people of God living in a pagan society over 2,500 years ago are still valid for us today as we undertake the task of living for God in an increasingly pagan society. I do know what we should be doing in the meantime.

The Commands
1. Build.
Some years ago, I was hired to go door-to-door collecting information for the national census that the government takes every ten years here in Canada. One young man stands

out in my mind. He boasted that he had not paid income tax in seven years. He didn't care that the census would help direct the spending of money to tasks such as electing political representatives, building roads, establishing schools and planning medical care. He was quite willing to use the roads, schools, hospitals and other services provided by society. But he had no interest in helping to provide those services. He was a user, a drain on his society's resources. I met many other people who were living productive lives, working hard, paying taxes, helping their neighbors, giving to the poor and volunteering time to various churches, charities and service organizations.

I learned the importance of hard work from my parents. My father worked a fifty-to-sixty-hour week and then came home and spent a couple of hours each evening working in our huge garden. He took two weeks' vacation each year and spent one of them painting or fixing up our house or doing other work around home. I think that is why my wife and I have a vegetable garden each year. We are not great gardeners, and our produce will never win any awards, but I derive an exaggerated sense of satisfaction from knowing that we are contributing at least something to the collective food supply that we all rely on to keep us alive and healthy.

There are essentially two types of people in the world. There are those who contribute, build, leave something positive behind, leave the world a better place. There are also those who consume and destroy, who take away from the collective wealth, who leave the world a worse place than they found it.

God's command through Jeremiah to "build houses and settle down; plant gardens and eat what they produce" (Jeremiah 29:5) is still valid today. It is an extension of the responsibility given to the first human beings, who were placed in the Garden of Eden "to work it and take care of it" (Genesis 2:15). All human beings have a responsibility to work, to first provide for their own needs and then also provide for the needs of others. This concept is repeated in the New Testament. Paul taught the Thessalonians to work, referring to his own example of working to support himself even though he could have used the excuse that he was too busy preaching about Jesus: "In the name of the Lord Jesus Christ, we command you, brothers and sisters, to keep away from every brother who is idle...For you yourselves know how you ought to follow our example. We were not idle when we were with you, nor did we eat anyone's food without paying for it. On the contrary, we worked night and day, laboring and toiling so that we would not be a burden to any of you. We did this, not because we do not have the right to such help, but in order to offer ourselves as a model for you to imitate. For even when we were with you, we gave you this rule: 'The one who is unwilling to work shall not eat.' We hear that some among you are idle. They are not busy; they are busybodies. Such people we command and urge in the Lord Jesus Christ to settle down and earn the bread they eat. And as for you, brothers and sisters, never tire of doing what is good" (2 Thessalonians 3:6-13). Paul also told the Ephesians: "Anyone who has been stealing must steal no longer, but must work, doing something useful with their own hands, that they may have something to share with those in need" (Ephesians 4:28).

Human beings were made to work. And however much we may dream of lying on a beach or retiring to a life of luxury, people who have done this often find it unsatisfying. Even if we are so wealthy that we don't need more money, we still need to work. We need to have a purpose. There is no shortage of work that needs to be done in the world, more often a shortage of workers. If you do not need money, volunteer for one of the many social agencies or charitable organizations that is crying out for help. In one of His parables, Jesus said, "The harvest is plentiful, but the workers are few" (Matthew 9:35-38, Luke 10:2).

2. Have children.

It is very easy to take having children for granted. We talk of "unwanted children" as if they represent a vast surplus of some worthless commodity. But the command to have children is a call to recognize the sacredness of human life. Human beings are the most precious thing on earth, the culmination of all that God created (Genesis 1:26-31), precious enough that God would sacrifice His Son to save them. Yet we in North American society do not value children. In our society, we see children as a nuisance and a hindrance to our own desires for self-fulfillment and pleasure. So, we abort them before they are born, dump them as soon as possible into daycare or some government institution and embrace mercy killing if they become incapacitated. In our world, human life is cheap, with millions dying needlessly due to preventable illness and preventable violence.

We assume that population grows automatically. It does not. Throughout history, population has grown in many times and places, but declined in other times and places. The birth rate and the population decline in societies that have no hope. The birth rate in North America has been dropping for decades due to an epidemic of despair and selfishness—we have no hope for the future, and we don't want to be bothered in the present. The birth rate is higher among immigrants who come to North America with hope, but dropping among established North Americans who have it all and have found it unsatisfying.

The future is uncertain, and we may well question whether we want to bring children into a world like ours, full of immorality, violence and suffering. The Jews 600 years before Christ might well have asked the same question. Their children would be born in exile and poverty, born subjects of a brutal dictator. Ours will be born subjects of a free and wealthy society. Yet the Jews produced children in accordance with God's command, and often we do not. Abraham and Sarah, Elkanah and Hannah, Zechariah and Elizabeth all fulfilled God's command to have children, and

God used their children for mighty purposes, to bless all people on earth. Having children is an act of hope and faith, hope that the world will be a safe place for them and faith that God will make their lives meaningful. Having children is an expression of faith that the God who tells us to have children will take care of them and that He has a purpose for them.

I am struck again by the fact that God's command was not primarily to have children. It was to "marry and have sons and daughters." God was not talking about producing children but about producing families. Children can be the result of a momentary act of selfishness and lust, a result of lack of self-control. We have an epidemic of people in North America having sex outside marriage, "accidentally" producing children and then abdicating all responsibility for raising them. What God was talking about was marriage and family, a deliberate lifetime commitment of a man and a woman to stay together, love each other and raise children.

Raising children, really raising them as they should be raised, is the ultimate act of unselfishness. It means endless hard work, sleepless nights, grief and worry. Good parents put more into raising their children than they ever get out. Raising children is an investment in the future of the world, an investment that will produce untold benefits for others, not necessarily benefits for the people who do it. God's first command through Jeremiah's letter was to build things for the future and leave the world a better place. Good children are the most important thing we can build and leave behind for the benefit of the world of human beings and the purposes of God.

Not everyone who wants to marries. Some wonderful Christians never find a spouse, and some wonderful Christian couples are never able to produce children. For them, this command may be a source of frustration. It need not be. God's statement that it is not good for a man to live alone (Genesis 2:18) goes beyond marriage itself. There are many ways to invest in people, to work for the building of the Kingdom of God. Many single people have done great work as school teachers and Sunday school teachers and missionaries and policemen and storekeepers and aunts and uncles. In the popular jargon, it takes a village to raise a child. The command God gave through Jeremiah was collective, not individual. It was to produce a stable society, where children were valued and raised properly and safely, where people were valued and loved.

We don't produce stable marriages and raise good children because in our society we are focused on instant gratification and personal pleasure. We need to have a far broader vision than that. We need to see things from God's perspective. We need to focus not on ourselves but on building the future Kingdom of God. The Jews who went into exile were to produce children so they in turn could produce children who might eventually find their way back to the Promised Land and restore the kingdom of God's people. A friend of mine was teaching about this concept once in a Sunday school class. A man who was visiting the class said he understood completely. He worked in silviculture, the replanting of trees after forests have been logged. He said he was spending his entire lifetime planting trees, none of which he would ever see harvested. His whole life's work was spent in producing something that only future generations could use. The great cathedrals of Europe took decades, sometimes centuries to build. Three or four or more generations of a family of stonemasons might spend their lifetimes building a cathedral so that their descendants would have a place to worship. Yet we want to achieve something immediately, to see the results of our labor. As we contemplate our lives here on earth, we need to have a broader vision. We need to commit ourselves to building the eternal Kingdom of God.

3. Seek the peace and prosperity of pagan society.

As it was for the Jews 2,600 years ago, this may be the hardest part of God's command for us to accept. Immersed as we are in the North American culture wars, it may seem incomprehensible to us that we should love and pray for the misguided politicians, the purveyors of violent and pornographic images and the social theorists whose policies undermine family life. These people don't deserve our prayers or God's salvation—but which of us sinners does? It is very easy to see these people as our enemies—instead of seeing them as pawns in the hands of Satan. It is very tempting to withdraw from the pagan society around us, to withdraw into our Christian schools, Christian books and Christian communities and let the world descend into the divine punishment it deserves. It is very awkward to keep being involved and giving our input in a society that wants us to shut up and go away. Daniel could understand that, because he had political enemies who did not want him around either. It is very tempting to withdraw from society and take care of our own, raising our children in a safe place where the world cannot touch them. But as Daniel's parents discovered, no matter how much the world might want us to be silent, the world will not let our children alone. We cannot live in splendid isolation from the pagan society around us because we live in it and we are inextricably bound up with its future. If it prospers, we will prosper. If it descends into a chaotic nightmare, we will suffer too. There is no wilderness refuge, no fortified bunker we can retreat to where the society around us cannot find us.

Besides, that is not what we are called to do. God's command is for us to "seek the peace and prosperity" of the society we find ourselves in and to "pray for it" (Jeremiah 29:7). These commands are repeated for Christians in the New Testament. Paul wrote, "I urge, then, first of all, that requests, prayers, intercession and thanksgiving be made for all people—for kings and all those in authority, that we may live peaceful and quiet lives in all godliness and holiness" (1 Timothy 2:1-2). This command comes with a similar promise to the promise in Jeremiah's command. We need to pray for government authorities because if there is good government, we Christians will be protected and be able to do the good work that we are supposed to be doing. If our society has peace and prosperity, we will have peace and prosperity. We might think that some of our rulers are so ungodly that they are beyond our prayers and our support. But the command to Jeremiah was given at a time when the cruel, arrogant Nebuchadnezzar was king, and the New Testament command was given at a time when the world was ruled by people like King Herod and the Roman emperors. Moreover, the command was not directed solely to rulers. Paul's command was to pray for "all people." Paul went on to say that we should be like God, "who wants all people to be saved" (1 Timothy 2:3-4). Paul himself was an apostle to the Gentiles, those hated and despised enemies of his own people.

The early Christian church followed the commands laid down by God. The early Christians could not change the standard practice of people abandoning unwanted babies, so they went out into the woods and rescued these abandoned children. They lived in a society where slavery was legal, so they urged that slaves be treated well, that slaves be freed (1 Timothy 1:10, 1 Corinthians 7:21, Philemon 1:16) and that slaves be treated as equal brothers in Christ (Philemon 1:16, 1 Corinthians 7:22, 12:13, Galatians 3:28, Colossians 3:11). They lived in a society where the poor were oppressed, so they fed the hungry and clothed the naked. They lived in a sexually corrupt era, so they taught sexual purity (Galatians 5:16-21, Ephesians 5:3), changed lives (1 Corinthians 6:11) and rescued prostitutes. They lived in a corrupt society where they did not set the rules, but they turned that society upside down.

Being a Daniel in our society means that we work very hard to make it a better society. This does not necessarily mean that we should seek a high government position like the one Daniel had or that seizing government power is the only way we can change society. Daniel had a very high government position but found that he couldn't on his own change government policy; that is why he had to chastise Nebuchadnezzar for his unjust social policies (Daniel 4:27). We should also remember that the command through

Jeremiah was not given to Daniel alone but to all of the thousands of Jewish exiles. Most of them never had a government position but lived as poor foreign exiles with no power and no influence. All most of them could do is quietly do their work and pray—but the fact is that many of them did their work and prayed. Maybe there is not a lot we can do, but we can do something. If nothing else, we can quietly do our work and pray.

This also does not mean that we accept the status quo and go along with things that are evil. Daniel did his job well and efficiently, but he was also not afraid to expose, confront and condemn evil, even when it put his own life in danger (for example, Daniel 4:27). There were many things he could not change, and there are no doubt many things that we cannot change in our society. Maybe we are unequal to the overwhelming negative and destructive forces that are tearing our society apart—but that is all the more reason to provide a counter-force that will build up what others are tearing down. And if we are unequal to the task, then we will have to rely more on the God we serve, who is more than equal to the forces of evil

4. Don't be misled by false prophecies.

Years ago, I encountered a church which was being forced into an expensive building program. The church had a fairly new building, but it was falling down and needed to be completely replaced. The church had developed out of a revival which had included a strong element of millennial expectations. The church members had expected Jesus to return very soon, so they had thrown up a building with shoddy materials and poor workmanship because they hadn't expected that it would have to last more than ten years. They had been wrong, and now they had to rebuild. I knew a member of that congregation. He had a keen mind and was a devout Christian. I liked him a lot and respected him greatly. But, coming out of this revival, he had expected the soon return of Jesus, so he had seen no need of getting an education or developing a trade. He had drifted through life, waiting for the end. Now, at retirement age, he was struggling to put food on the table, and he looked back on a life in which he hadn't accomplished very much.

In Matthew 24, Jesus taught His followers to "keep watch, because you do not know on what day your Lord will come" (Matthew 24:42). We are to be ready, waiting for Jesus to come again. But how are we supposed to "keep watch"? What does that look like? Jesus went on to explain: "Who then is the faithful and wise servant, whom the master has put in charge of the servants in his household to give them their food at the proper time? It will be good for that servant whose master finds him doing so when he returns" (Matthew 24:45-46). The same teaching is presented in Mark 13:32-27, where Jesus talked about each servant having his "assigned task," and in Luke 12:35-48, where Jesus said servants should be "dressed ready for service." All of these passages warn against sleeping and neglecting one's duty. In Luke 17:7-10, Jesus emphasized that it is the duty of servants to serve. In the parable of the ten minas (Luke 19:11-27), Jesus emphasized the importance of putting to work the gifts and talents He has given us, instead of playing it safe, taking no risks and hoarding our resources.

There are many churches today which take a great interest in prophecy. They study biblical prophecy in depth to discern who the King of the South is and when the end times will come. There are other churches which take no interest in prophecy, assuming that Jesus will not return for a long time yet. I am not going to pretend to know which group is right. Whether Jesus comes today or thousands of years from now makes no practical difference in my duty. My job as a servant of the Most High God is to serve, to build a better world, to produce physical and spiritual children of God, to work and pray for the peace and prosperity of the lost world around me, to do all I can to build the Kingdom of God. If Jesus comes tomorrow, I want Him to find me working for Him. If He does not come for a long time, I want to spend my life working for Him. The study of biblical prophecy is important, but it should always spur us to do the things we have been commanded to do, never distract us from our duty.

There are false uses of biblical prophecy. There are people who are so preoccupied with studying the end times and the coming of the Kingdom of God that they do absolutely nothing to help bring that Kingdom. There are Christians who are convinced that the world is inevitably getting worse, that the Great Tribulation is coming and that they will be raptured out of that Tribulation. Some of these people are so convinced of this interpretation of biblical prophecy that they are content to watch the world around them descend into hell without lifting a finger to help, without attempting to save even a few souls from the fire. Six hundred years before Christ, the Jews faced the very real temptation of false prophecy that would distract them from undertaking the lifetime of hard work that God was calling them to do. We face the same temptation today, the danger of letting prophecy distract us from our duty.

Seventy years was a long time to wait for the promised return to the Jewish homeland. Seventy years is also a lifetime, the average length of time people live (Psalm 90:10). In a pagan society, this is the fourth lifetime commitment we need to make:

I will seek the peace and prosperity of the society in which I live.

Chapter 7
Hanging in over the Long Haul
Daniel 5

The New King

Here again we have evidence that the Bible, and the book of Daniel in particular, was written to reveal the nature of God and not to provide a thorough history of Daniel or any other human being. A great deal of Babylonian history has been passed over in silence. The story told in Daniel 5 took place in 539 BC, sixty-six years after Daniel and his friends were taken into captivity and at least twenty years after the events related in chapter 4.

In the meantime, Nebuchadnezzar had died, in 562 BC, after a glorious reign lasting more than forty years. The next few years were marked by a vicious power struggle. Nebuchadnezzar was succeeded by his son Amel-Marduk (sometimes called Evil-Merodach), which means "The man is Marduk" (Marduk was one of the Babylonian gods). The ancient historian Josephus said that Amel-Marduk ruled "lawlessly and wantonly." He was killed in 560 by his brother-in-law, Neriglissar (Nergal-Sharezer, "O Nergal, protect the king," mentioned in Jeremiah 39:3 and possibly 39:13 as one of the Babylonian commanders who destroyed Jerusalem). Neriglissar was succeeded only four years later by his son, Labashi-Marduk, who was quickly replaced after only nine months, in 556 BC, by Nabonidus, another of

Nebuchadnezzar's sons. Nabonidus ruled for seventeen years but was apparently not popular with his subjects. For much of his reign, he was off fighting in Arabia, so he left the administration of Babylon to Belshazzar, his son and therefore Nebuchadnezzar's grandson. In this chapter, Nebuchadnezzar is said to be Belshazzar's "father" (Daniel 5:2,11,13), but the term is not precise. Like the English term, it can sometimes mean "ancestor."

Belshazzar is a central character in this chapter, so it is worth taking time to look at him. While Nebuchadnezzar was a great conqueror and builder, and while Nabonidus was away at war, Belshazzar stayed in Babylon. No buildings or other accomplishments are attributed to him. All we know about him is this one incident, a feast which, from the repeated mentions of it, seems to have focused on drinking wine. Belshazzar goes down in history as a drunk.

But we know something else about him. Balshazzar followed the traditional Babylonian religion. He worshiped the Babylonian gods, represented by statues made "of gold and silver, of bronze, iron, wood and stone" (Daniel 5:4,23). The parallel with the statue of Nebuchadnezzar's dream in chapter 2 is no accident. The point is that these gods were manmade, and also that they were declining in value, from gold to wood and stone. As Daniel pointed out (Daniel 5:23), there was no real god, no power, behind these representations. They were unequal to the real God, who is so great and powerful that He cannot be represented adequately by a statue and who therefore insists that no such statues be made.

Furthermore, Belshazzar made a point of drinking toasts to the false Babylonian gods from the gold and silver goblets taken from the temple of the true God, Yahweh, in Jerusalem. He and his nobles had already been drinking, so he did not send for those goblets because he had run short of drinking utensils. It was not an unthinking momentary lapse in judgment. His action was a deliberate insult to Yahweh, a demonstration of Belshazzar's long-held belief that the

Babylonian gods were superior to Yahweh. It was a challenge that the true God did not ignore. He wrote His response on Belshazzar's wall.

Belshazzar further demonstrated his traditional Babylonian beliefs by consulting the "enchanters, astrologers and diviners" (Daniel 5:7) to explain the mysterious writing that had suddenly appeared on the wall of his banquet hall.

It was at this point that "the queen," hearing the commotion, entered the hall. It is not stated who she was. She was not Belshazzar's wife. His wives and concubines were already there, drinking wine with him (Daniel 5:2,3). She might have been the wife of Nabonidus, the true current king, in which case she could have been Belshazzar's mother. Or she could have been the wife of Nebuchadnezzar. In this case, she would probably not have been the foreign (Median) wife for whom he had built the famous hanging gardens—that woman would most likely have been dead by then. But this queen may well have been a later wife of Nebuchadnezzar. She certainly knew that "the spirit of the holy gods" (Daniel 4:8,9,18) was in Daniel and that Daniel's God was more powerful than the Babylonian gods. She made a point of stating that Daniel had formerly been appointed head of the Babylonian magicians, enchanters, astrologers and diviners who had failed to explain the writing on the wall for Belshazzar. She seems to have been suggesting that Daniel's God was superior to the Babylonian religions. It is a logical conclusion that she was a follower of the true God, as Daniel and Nebuchadnezzar were.

It is interesting that the queen called Daniel by his Jewish name. Now it might be argued that it would be awkward to call him by his Babylonian name, Belteshazzar, which was so close to the new king's name. But Nebuchadnezzar also in his final years had reverted to sometimes calling Daniel by his original name (Daniel 4:8,19). It was a recognition that Daniel's God had not been conquered by the Babylonian gods but that Daniel's God had proven to be superior to the Babylonian gods.

There is also no mistaking the queen's contempt for Belshazzar. She repeated Nebuchadnezzar's title as king (Daniel 5:11) for emphasis. (The New American Standard Bible translates her words literally: "King Nebuchadnezzar, your father, your father the king.") It is as if she was saying, "Nebuchadnezzar was a king, but you are not." Perhaps it was a jibe at Belshazzar for claiming the title of king even though he was really only a chief administrator for his father, King Nabonidus.

When Daniel came in, Belshazzar made a point of putting him in his place. He reminded Daniel that Daniel was an exile, a foreigner, one of the people that Nebuchadnezzar had conquered. It was Belshazzar's way of saying that he was better than Daniel. However, he did offer Daniel the third place in the kingdom (after Nabonidus and Belshazzar) if he could interpret the mysterious handwriting.

Daniel was not impressed. Daniel seems to have respected Nebuchadnezzar and even to have developed a friendship with him, although Daniel never seems to have used the over-elaborate greetings of others, such as "May the king live forever!" (Daniel 5:10). However, there seems to be no suggestion of respect here. Daniel bluntly refused the king's offered rewards. (He knew Belshazzar would not be around long enough to make good on his offer anyway.) But Daniel also expressed no regret for God's coming judgment on Belshazzar. There was no statement here of "if only the dream applied to your enemies" which Daniel had expressed when Nebuchadnezzar had faced judgment (Daniel 4:19). There was no urging to repent and avoid condemnation, such as Daniel had given to Nebuchadnezzar (Daniel 4:27).

The Message

Even in their drunken haze, seeing the disembodied fingers of a hand suddenly appearing was understandably terrifying for Belshazzar and his friends. It was something clearly supernatural, like something out of a modern horror movie. No wonder Belshazzar called for his magicians to interpret not only the meaning of the words but also the meaning of this bizarre event—since they were supposed experts in the supernatural, it should have been something that was in their area of expertise. The passage says that the fingers wrote the message on the plaster of the wall. Nothing is said of a pen. The words were possibly carved into the plaster of the wall, similar to the common form of Babylonian writing, which consisted of letters carved into wet clay, which then hardened and preserved the writing. It is also reminiscent of Yahweh writing His covenant, which we know as the Ten Commandments, on stone tablets (Exodus 32:15-16). The first of those Commandments was the one that Belshazzar had just violated so deliberately: "You shall have no other gods before me" (Exodus 20:3). Incidentally, remnants of plaster walls have been found in the ruins of the royal palaces in Babylon.

The Babylonian magicians could not interpret the writing or the phenomenon of its appearance on the wall. Daniel could—or rather Daniel's God could, because He is the One who had done the writing. The magicians said that they could not read and interpret the writing, yet the words of the message were clear enough. They were apparently written in Chaldean, the native language of the Babylonians. They were *mene* (numbered), *tekel* (weighed) and *peres* (divided). Since ancient money was made of weighed and measured precious metals, these words also referred to units of currency. It was as if God had written "dollar, quarter, dime" on a modern wall. The *mene* (remember the parable of the ten minas in Luke 19:11-27) was a large measure of money, in the general range of thousands of dollars, and contained fifty or sixty shekels (or *tekels*). A *peres* was half a shekel. Note that the coins were listed in decreasing order of value. This suggested that Belshazzar's kingdom was declining and that Belshazzar (who only had half a kingdom since he was sharing the kingdom with his father) was not nearly the man Nebuchadnezzar had been. *Peres* was also a pun, similar to the word *paras*, Persian. It is not clear why *mene* was written twice or why *peres* was first cited in the plural, *parsim*.

If the words were clear, the meaning was not. That is why Daniel was needed to interpret the words. The message that God was sending Belshazzar was that He had judged (weighed and measured) Belshazzar and his kingdom and concluded that they deserved to be destroyed. It was a terrible judgment.

Belshazzar's response to the message is fascinating. On the one hand, he seems to have believed that Daniel had given him a correct interpretation of the message. This can be inferred from the fact that he gave Daniel the reward he had promised.

But there is another sense in which Belshazzar does not seem to have believed the message at all. If he really believed that his kingdom was about to be destroyed, he would have realized that giving Daniel a high position in his kingdom was a pointless act. Belshazzar, who had been terrified by the writing at first, now acted as if his kingdom was going to continue and he was still in charge. Perhaps he thought that since the message had apparently come from Israel's God and since Babylon had defeated Israel, then the Babylonian gods would be able to thwart God's plans. Perhaps he thought that, now that he had been warned, he himself could take some action to prevent his kingdom from falling to the Persians. He was blinded to reality by his own preconceived ideas.

The one action that possibly could have saved Belshazzar never seems to have occurred to him. Belshazzar could have repented, admitted that the God of Heaven (rather than the gods of the Babylonians) was the one true God, submitted himself to God and begged God to forgive him for his blasphemy and other sins. Belshazzar did not do this.

On first reading this story, I wondered whether God was being unfair. After all, He had given Nebuchadnezzar several visions and warnings over a number of years before that final humiliating experience that had changed him into a believer. Belshazzar, on the other hand, seems to have received only this one warning just hours before he died. God seems to have been far more patient with Nebuchadnezzar than with Belshazzar. But it must be remembered that Nebuchadnezzar responded positively, if not completely, to God's first intervention in his life. From his first encounter with God, Nebuchadnezzar began moving toward belief. Nebuchadnezzar struggled to change, but he was willing to accept the truth when he saw it. The opposite is true of Belshazzar. His first significant encounter with God was probably seeing what God had done with his grandfather Nebuchadnezzar. Belshazzar's response was to deliberately defy the one true God by using God's sacred cups to worship other gods. He deliberately chose to remember that Babylon had conquered Israel and to forget that Israel's God had conquered Babylon's gods. He had a selective memory. If we ask why Belshazzar wasn't given the same miraculous revelations, the answer is that he was given a very miraculous intervention and rejected it. It is interesting that the term "writing on the wall" has become a common modern phrase for a coming judgment that has become extremely obvious.

Furthermore, if Belshazzar had taken the trouble to investigate, he would have discovered that the sudden destruction of Babylon had been prophesied even earlier by God's prophets Isaiah and Jeremiah (Isaiah 13:1-14:23, Jeremiah 50-51). As well, Daniel himself had received a vision fourteen years earlier that the Persians would conquer Babylon (Daniel 8:1-4). This vision had been given in the third year of Belshazzar's reign. The vision placed Daniel in Susa, one of the leading cities of the Persians, at that time ruled by Babylon. It concerned a two-horned ram that would charge west (toward Babylon), the two horns, of course, representing the alliance of the Medes and Persians.

We shouldn't be misled by the fact that the book of Daniel has left out years of Babylonian history. Belshazzar was not a newly appointed king guilty of a single youthful mistake. Belshazzar and his father had been ruling Babylon for seventeen years. He had several wives. He had had many years to repent and had only used those years to confirm the direction he had determined to go. His final acts on his final night were a continuation of a whole lifetime of defiance of God. His life and his destruction are a reminder that God does not owe us infinite chances.

Belshazzar, like many modern people, made the mistake of thinking that he was in charge of his own life. He did not believe Daniel's message that God held Belshazzar's life in His hands (Daniel 5:23). Yet God had clearly demonstrated the truth of Daniel's assertion by coming into the palace, the symbol and center of Babylonian power, and writing on the wall.

The book of Daniel says that Daniel's prophecy was immediately fulfilled: "That very night, Belshazzar, king of the Babylonians, was slain, and Darius the Mede took over the kingdom" (5:30). One can understand Belshazzar's complacency. As described in chapter 1 of this book, the city of Babylon had massive defenses, and the army of the Medes and Persians seemingly had little hope of capturing it. Belshazzar probably knew that an invading army was outside the walls, but he was so unconcerned that he decided to hold a feast rather than supervise the city's defenses. Yet, ancient historians record that while the Babylonians were carousing at a feast to their gods, the Persian army diverted the flow of the Euphrates River and gained access to the city through the dry river bed with the help of some deserters. No matter how unlikely they seem, God's prophecies cannot be thwarted.

The Issues

It is interesting that the issues Daniel was dealing with near the end of his life in 539 BC were the same issues that he had dealt with when he had first gone into exile sixty-six years earlier.

The key question was: Who is God? Is God the human-like gods of the Babylonians, limited in power and knowledge and often acting immorally? Or is the true God the God who had revealed Himself to the Israelites, the God of infinite power, the moral God who demands that human beings be moral as well? Everything else follows from the answer to this question. If God is indeed all-powerful and moral, then it follows that He holds our life and all our ways in His hand (Daniel 5:23), that we are subject to His judgment. Our response should be to humble ourselves, submit to His power and authority and beg Him to forgive us for our failure to live up to His moral law. Our response should be to recognize that God is in charge and we are not.

Daniel was teaching the same things at the end of his life as at the beginning. However, as this chapter makes clear, some people accepted Daniel's message, and others did not. Their responses determined their fate. Yet, through it all, regardless of people's choices, God remained God.

This all seems so obvious to us, and, as modern North American Christians, we are quite confident that we will not make the mistake Belshazzar made. We are quite confident that we are worshiping the true God. But the attitude of Belshazzar is more insidious than we think. Are we absolutely convinced that God is all-powerful and that He can see the things that we think we have kept hidden, even sometimes from ourselves? More practically, how do we actually treat God? Do we really approach Him as if He is in charge or as if we are? Are we constantly aware that we live under the judgment of God, or do our thoughts focus on judging God, on determining whether He is treating us well enough for us to continue worshiping Him? In our Bible reading, do we look for "promises" that will give us the things we want, or do we look for God's commands so that we will do what He wants? Are we looking to use God to build our kingdoms, or are we willing to sacrifice ourselves to build His Kingdom? Are our prayers focused on finding God's will so that we can serve Him, or are our prayers long lists of requests that we are expecting God to fulfill? In our Christian life, who is really giving the orders? Before we dismiss Belshazzar, perhaps we should ponder whether we are more like him than we would like to admit. Wouldn't we really sometimes rather have a god of wood or stone that we can control?

Daniel's End

By the time of this story, Daniel must have been an old man. He had already been in exile about sixty-six years. He was quite possibly retired. He was no longer head of the wise men, and the king didn't even seem to know who he was. His many years of faithful, competent service and his miraculous interpretations of dreams seem to have been forgotten, at least by those now in power. All he had spent his life building up in the Babylonian Empire was about to be destroyed. His friend Nebuchadnezzar was dead, and a new king was in power whose policies he despised. No mention is made of his three friends, Hananiah, Mishael and Azariah, so it is possible that they also were dead. Perhaps worst of all, as an old man, Daniel knew that it was too late for him to return home to Jerusalem; he was too old to make that arduous journey and begin rebuilding a devastated city.

Is this how God rewards His faithful servants? Daniel could have been a bitter, lonely old man. He could have stopped serving God. He could have stopped telling people about a God they didn't want to believe in. He could have simply given in to tiredness and despair. But the fact is that we find Daniel remaining as faithful to God at the end of his life as he was at the beginning. He was still exercising his gifts. He was still proclaiming the message of the one true God, whether anybody listened or not. His old friends had died, but he had developed friendships with other people, possibly including the queen. (We don't know if they ever talked, but she knew he was alive and still active.)

So many of God's servants today don't finish well. Many retire and stop serving in the church just as they have stopped working at their jobs, even though they have more time now. Some stop telling others about Jesus—they conclude that they did that when they were young and, as is the case with earning a boy scout badge, they don't have to do it again. Or perhaps they have lost their enthusiasm for God. Tired from the battles of life, they have stopped fighting. Thinking they cannot change the downward spiral of a pagan society, they have stopped trying. Assuming they can no longer be tempted to sin, they have relaxed in their observation of the spiritual disciplines they have practiced for years. They have accepted the immorality of the young without protest. They may have become lonely and bitter and unpleasant. Some may have even deserted God altogether.

Satan does not take pity on the old and weak, or the young and foolish. We are immersed in the battle between good and evil all of our lives. There is no retirement. It is possible for us to lose our way in our last years. In a pagan society, this is the fifth commitment we need to make:

I will remain faithful to God's call, serving Him till the end of my life.

Chapter 8
Standing in the Need of Prayer
Daniel 6

The Setting

We should be careful not to read our modern political theory back into the past. We think in terms of the nation state, with the French people living in France, the German people living in Germany, the Spanish living in Spain, etc. The ancient Middle East was composed of a number of ethnic groups, but these groups did not each comprise a separate independent national state. Rather, the area was generally organized into an empire, with the leadership of the empire changing from time to time. Babylon, as we have mentioned, was centered in the Tigris and Euphrates valleys in what is now Iraq. For a time, the empire, including Babylon, was ruled by the Assyrians, who lived to the northwest of Babylon. Nebuchadnezzar's father rebelled against Assyrian rule and made Babylon a separate state. Nebuchadnezzar then re-established the empire, but with Babylon as its center. The Medes, a people to the northeast of Babylon, and the Persians, a people to the east of Babylon in what is now Iran, were part of the Babylonian Empire. What happened in Daniel 6 is that the Medes and the Persians joined forces, rebelled and defeated Babylon. They then re-established the empire under the leadership of the Medes and the Persians, with the Persians being the dominant partner. This is the context in which Daniel stated that "the Most High God is sovereign over all kingdoms on earth and sets over them anyone he wishes" (Daniel 5:21). God remained, the land and the people remained, but the political leaders were interchangeable.

Darius the Mede seems to have been given the authority to administer Babylon itself for the new Persian Empire. There is no mention of Darius outside the Bible. Some scholars have argued that Darius must be another name for Cyrus, the head of the Persian Empire. Others have argued that Darius could be another name for Gubaru, a general who was said to have conquered Babylon and who administered both Babylon and the area to the west. However, the fact is that most of the government records for that time have been lost and it is quite possible that a separate man named Darius ruled the province of Babylon. (This Darius should also not be confused with two other Dariuses, who later ruled the entire Persian Empire—Darius I, mentioned in the books of Ezra, Haggai and Zechariah, and Darius II, called Darius the Persian in the book of Nehemiah.)

As described in the previous chapter, the Medes and the Persians sneaked into the city of Babylon by night. They killed Belshazzar and no doubt many of the other Babylonian leaders (presumably the people at his drunken banquet). However, the city was not destroyed, and Darius simply took over the existing administrative structure. He would use many of the same administrators that the Babylonians had used since they knew how the system worked. These men, it should be remembered, were drawn from the many ethnic groups conquered by the Babylonians and could as easily serve the Persians as the Babylonians. It would have been similar to the changeover after an election in a democracy—the top administrators are replaced, but the rest of the bureaucracy remains intact, and even many of the top administrators are just shuffled from one position to another.

And so it was that Daniel was called out of retirement to be one of the top three administrators of the province of Babylon. It was possibly an interim arrangement, as the king waited to see which of the three administrators served the best. It also would not be expected that Daniel, an old man, would serve for a long time.

It is not at all surprising that Darius would appoint Daniel to this position. As a Jew, he would have been considered as not particularly loyal to the old Babylonian regime, which had pushed him into retirement anyway. It is also possible that Darius had heard of Daniel's role in the prophecy against Belshazzar on the night that Babylon was captured. But there is more to it than that. We might assume that the Persians didn't know anything about Daniel. But if we overlook the miraculous events of the earlier chapters of Daniel, the people of the time did not. Remember that the Medes and the Persians had been part of the Babylonian Empire. When King Nebuchadnezzar had called the leaders of all parts of his empire together to worship his golden statue, surely there were Median and Persian leaders among them. They would have witnessed the intervention of the Most High God overpowering the Babylonian gods to rescue His servants Hananiah, Mishael and Azariah. Nebuchadnezzar's decree that no one should speak against this Most High God (Daniel 3:29) would have been proclaimed also in Media and Persia. Similarly, Nebuchadnezzar's proclamation of how he had been humbled by the Most High God and His servant Daniel had been sent all over the Babylonian Empire (Daniel 4:1). We are used to believers being overlooked and ignored in our society, but Daniel and his God would have been very well known to Darius and the rest of the Medes and the Persians. Daniel's appointment to administer Babylon is evidence that the miraculous stories in the first chapters of the book of Daniel were still remembered and are therefore true.

Office Politics

The story in Daniel 6 probably took place within a year or so of Darius becoming ruler of Babylon in 539 BC. There had been enough time for him to put the new administration into place and to start to think about what he wanted to do in the long run, but the situation was still somewhat in flux. It was a crucial time when it was still being determined what direction the new regime would take.

It is fascinating to look at this story through the actions and attitudes of the main characters.

First, the satraps and administrators come across as thoroughly corrupt. They had no loyalty to any regime. Their primary purpose was to use their positions for their own benefit. They would no doubt use all of the tools that dishonest administrators have used throughout the centuries. They would embezzle funds, accept bribes, give favors to friends. It is interesting that King Darius was aware of such sinful human tendencies. He had appointed three administrators precisely to prevent the 120 satraps from acting dishonestly. Unfortunately, two of the administrators were as corrupt as he feared the satraps were.

These satraps and administrators were also very adept at office politics. They knew how to curry favor and eliminate rivals in order to move up the corporate ladder. They could not find any just way to discredit Daniel, so they invented a new crime, making one of Daniel's virtues illegal. They then lied to the king, saying that all of the administrators and satraps had agreed in recommending the new law, when in fact one of the top three administrators (Daniel) did not even know about it. In essence, they were attempting to perpetrate a judicial murder. They were going to kill Daniel in order to further their own political careers. In the end, they were justly executed for gross corruption and attempted murder.

The administrators were also racially prejudiced. Daniel had been a faithful administrator in Babylon for decades, and he was now one of the top bureaucrats in the province. But they did not describe him as "Daniel the administrator." To them, he was "one of the exiles from Judah" (Daniel 6:13), a foreigner, not "one of us."

Further, these satraps and administrators seem to have been thoroughly pagan and irreligious. Perhaps they were disillusioned skeptics, atheists (believing there is no God) or agnostics (believing that the existence of God is unprovable, unimportant and irrelevant). They seem to have practiced no religion, to have espoused no great principles. They saw religion as just one more tool to use in their office infighting. The text does not say that all 120 satraps were involved in the plot, although it is safe to assume that the other two top administrators were. It is hard to imagine all 122 of them coming to the king or going as a group to catch Daniel at prayer. It is doubtful that 122 officials and their families would have fit into the lions' den. We can only speculate on the attitude of those bureaucrats not involved in the plot. Did they secretly support it? Did they refuse to dirty their hands with it while secretly hoping it would succeed? (Any vacancy at the top would create the opportunity for them all to move up one notch.) Did they think the administrators' actions were wrong but not blow the whistle because they were afraid of the administrators and didn't want to risk their own jobs and lives? Were some of them as honest and trustworthy as Daniel and just didn't know about the plot?

Similar bureaucratic corruption exists in modern governments and businesses. Modern employees face the same questions and choices as the bureaucrats in Daniel's time. Will they see their positions as opportunities to contribute to building a healthy society, or will they use their positions to serve their own purposes? Will they accept bribes, show favoritism, embezzle money? Will they devise plots, invent lies and sacrifice other people to get ahead in the seamy world of office politics? Will they prove "trustworthy and neither corrupt nor negligent" (Daniel 6:5)?

Blinded by Power

King Darius comes off looking somewhat better than the administrators and satraps. He appreciated Daniel's honesty and competence, and he was going to give a promotion based on merit. He wanted to act justly, both in sparing Daniel's life and in punishing the other administrators (although punishing the administrators' families was unjust). He was also anxious to abide by the law, even when it did not suit him. Unlike the administrators, he also seems to have had respect for Daniel's God (Daniel 6:16,20,25-27).

But Darius had a serious flaw. Like many rulers, he had become arrogant. This made him susceptible to flattery. The proposed law that no one could pray to any god or human being other than Darius might have seemed to him a useful tool to use to consolidate his power in the newly conquered Babylon. It declared that he, rather than the former Babylonian regime, was in charge and thus discouraged loyalty to the remnants of the old rulers. It forbade worship of the old Babylonian gods. But the law's main thrust was to flatter Darius. It was a declaration that he was superior to all other human beings, and to the gods as well. That may not have mattered when it came to the Babylonian gods of gold and wood. But it was a huge mistake to claim superiority over the living God in whom Daniel believed.

The idea that the laws of the Medes and Persians could never be changed seems ludicrous to us. We change laws all the time. However, the concept is similar to the power of precedent in our legal system or to the profound respect given to the US constitution. It was an attempt to maintain equality and justice—the same laws were to apply to everyone at all times and couldn't be changed to offer special favors. But the idea also carries with it a strain of arrogance. It assumes that the Persian rulers were infallible, that they could never make a mistake or enact unjust laws. As the law Darius enacted clearly demonstrates, this was not the case. As sinful human beings, the Persian rulers could no more claim infinite wisdom and absolute morality than any other human being. And as for the laws of the Medes and Persians never being changed, it is a fact that the Median and Persian laws and the Median and Persian rulers have long since faded into history. It is only God's law that remains forever.

Daniel

When Christians talk about glorifying God "on the job," they sometimes take a narrow view. Some will focus on "witnessing," talking to their co-workers about God. Others focus on being scrupulously moral. Daniel shows what the complete life of a believer in the true God should look like.

In the first place, he was highly competent. He showed such "exceptional qualities" that King Darius, after only a short time on the job, decided to promote him to chief administrator (Daniel 6:3). Those who conspired against him could find no flaws in his conduct of government affairs (Daniel 6:4). He was an old man, tired after long years of service, but he still worked hard—he was not "negligent" (Daniel 6:4).

Second, Daniel was highly moral. In chapter 1 of the book of Daniel, we found him and his friends, alone of all the exiles and other government employees, determined to live morally. Sixty-six years later, nothing had changed in this regard. While the rest of the government bureaucracy was full of corruption, Daniel was still trustworthy and not corrupt (Daniel 6:4). Many people start out with high ideals; then, over time, they become tired and disillusioned; they despair of making a difference or of maintaining a perfect record; small compromises lead to larger compromises; and they end mired in deep corruption. This is seen in the man who has been faithful to his wife for twenty-five years and then leaves her for a younger woman. It is seen in the employee who has been a good employee but then embezzles money to finance a better retirement. Daniel lived a remarkably consistent life. And even when his long years of faithful service were rewarded by being unjustly thrown into a den of lions, there is no hint that he was bitter.

Third, Daniel had retained his deep commitment to the living God. He did not seem to annoy people with constant "God talk," but he also did not hide his faith in God. Beginning with his interpretation of Nebuchadnezzar's dream in chapter 2, he was willing to forthrightly tell people about the living God, even pagans who might not be expected to be very receptive to his statements. He had even been willing to tell people, graciously, lovingly and humbly, that God did not approve of some of the things that they were doing. No matter how unwelcome his statements, people were willing to listen to Daniel. We may think that this was because of the miracles that God did for him. But the miracles often came later. Initially, people listened to Daniel's witness about God because they respected him. Even his enemies admitted that he was a good worker, a moral man and a sincere believer. He lived a consistently devout life.

The Outcome

Asiatic lions (similar to African lions) lived wild throughout the ancient Middle East, although they have now been reduced to a small enclave in India. Because of their power, they were considered a royal animal. As noted in chapter 1 of this book, larger-than-life carvings of lions, bulls and dragons decorated the walls of the great Processional Way that led from the main city gate into the heart of Babylon. Many ancient kings bred lions in captivity, including the Assyrians before the Babylonians. The particular lions in Daniel 6 were probably left over from the Babylonian regime. (In the vision of Daniel 7, the lion was used as a symbol of the Babylonian Empire.) Besides being a symbol of royal power, the lions were used as a handy means of execution. The terror of this form of death was part of the deterrent effect of the punishment. Cruel punishments were not unusual in the past. We may remember that the Roman Emperors had Christians and notorious criminals publicly executed by lions in an arena.

It was evidently customary for Persian rulers to also execute the families of those guilty of serious crimes. This also was part of the deterrent. Those contemplating wrongdoing might think twice if they knew their families would also suffer. (Of course, having been castrated by the Babylonians, Daniel had no family.) The fact that the lions began devouring the conspirators and their families before they reached the floor of the den proves the lions were ravenously hungry. This means that it was not luck but divine intervention that had saved Daniel. Like the deliverance of Hananiah, Mishael and Azariah from the furnace in Daniel 3, this miraculous deliverance demonstrated the superior power of the one true God over the symbol of the power of the Babylonians and Persians. No wound was found on Daniel (Daniel 6:23), just as not even a hair was singed on Hananiah, Mishael and Azariah (Daniel 3:27).

We might note in passing that the rigorous Persian adherence to the law, which resulted in Daniel being thrown into the lions' den, also led to his release. The punishment was carried out literally. The punishment was "to be thrown into the lions' den," not "to be killed by lions." Daniel was thrown into the lions' den. That he was able to walk out the next morning did not negate the fact that the punishment had been carried out. If the conspirators and their families had been still alive the day after being thrown into the lions' den, perhaps they would have been allowed to walk out too. We do not know if there was any convention for how long a person was required to stay in a lions' den. The question must have rarely come up before, if ever. However, many legal systems provide for release if execution fails. It is a provision intended to allow for divine deliverance of an unjustly convicted person.

In this case, Daniel's God had clearly intervened, and Darius issued a proclamation, similar to Nebuchadnezzar's proclamations in chapters 3 and 4. The proclamation praised the power of Daniel's God. It declared that Daniel's God was "living" (Daniel 6:26, in contrast to the pagan idols). It even picked up the imagery from Daniel 2 of God's Kingdom enduring forever. It mentioned the signs and wonders God had performed in recent years, a reference to more than Daniel's delivery from the lions. Like Nebuchadnezzar's proclamations, it commanded respect for Daniel's God, although no enforcement mechanisms or threatened punishments for violation were mentioned. It seems a genuine statement of Darius's respect for Daniel's God. Had he, like Nebuchadnezzar, become a committed follower of Yahweh? We do not know. All we know is that, like Nebuchadnezzar, Darius was impressed by God and declared that respect to the nations.

What is also worthy of note is that the true God had not changed. Time had passed, and a new empire had arisen, but God was still declaring His glory and morality to a new empire. God speaks to every new generation, and every new generation has to learn who God is and how He should be worshiped.

God's miraculous deliverance of Daniel may have also played a role in another development. As mentioned earlier, we do not know who Darius was exactly. He might have been appointed head of the province of Babylon, under the rule of Cyrus, emperor of the Persian Empire. The Bible says that Daniel "prospered during the reign of Darius and the reign of Cyrus the Persian" (Daniel 6:28). This seems to suggest that Cyrus followed Darius as king, but we know that Cyrus had already been ruling for a long time and had conquered Media by 550 BC (he himself was related to the royal house of the Medes), and this was eleven years before the Medes and Persians conquered Babylon. Why then does Daniel 6:28 suggest that Daniel prospered under the reigns of the two men, as if they ruled at separate times rather than at the same time? The ancient historian Josephus (not always a reliable source) stated that three years after he began serving under Darius in Babylon, Daniel was moved to Media or Persia. This does not mean that Daniel was punished and sent into exile. It is more likely that Daniel was promoted from service in the province of Babylon to service in Media or in Persia, the new center of the empire. Perhaps Daniel became an influential administrator in the Persian Empire, as he had been an influential administrator in the Babylonian Empire.

This is interesting because:

> In the first year of Cyrus king of Persia, in order to fulfill the word of the LORD spoken by Jeremiah, the LORD moved the heart of Cyrus king of Persia to make a proclamation throughout his realm and also to put it in writing: 'This is what Cyrus king of Persia says: "The LORD, the God of heaven, has given me all the kingdoms of the earth and he has appointed me to build a temple for him at Jerusalem in Judah. Any of his people among you may go up to Jerusalem in Judah and build the temple of the LORD, the God of Israel, the God who is in Jerusalem, and may their God be with them. And in any locality where survivors may now be living, the people are to provide them with silver and gold, with goods and livestock, and with freewill offerings for the temple of God in Jerusalem."' (Ezra 1:1-4, 2 Chronicles 36:22-23)

One of the first things Cyrus did after overcoming the Babylonian Empire and establishing his own was to free the Jews to return from exile to their own land. It was Daniel's dream come true. Several things about this proclamation are remarkable. First, the Bible says that the LORD (God's name, Yahweh) moved Cyrus to do this. How did God do this? By a miraculous overpowering of Cyrus's will? It is interesting that Cyrus identified Yahweh as "the God of heaven," the phrase that Daniel used throughout the book of Daniel to distinguish the true God from the very earthly gods of the Babylonians. Cyrus also acknowledged that it was Yahweh who had given him his empire. This is the message that

Daniel and his friends had been proclaiming throughout the book of Daniel.

Historians tell us that the Persian Empire reversed the policy of the Babylonian Empire. Whereas the Babylonians had moved conquered peoples out of their traditional homelands in order to discourage rebellion, the Persians thought it wiser to leave the peoples of their empire in their traditional homelands (and even to send them back to their traditional homelands). Because of this, the Persians assumed, the peoples would be grateful to the Persian emperors and not *want* to rebel. It was a far more humane and generous policy. The policy did not just apply to the Jews. (And there is a hint in Cyrus's proclamation that he thought Yahweh might be just the God of the Jews and the God of Jerusalem and not the God of the whole world.) But there is more to it than that. In acknowledging that Yahweh had given him his empire, Cyrus was also acknowledging that he had an obligation to rule according to Yahweh's commands. A humane policy would certainly be in accordance with Yahweh's commands.

If we ask how Cyrus knew about Yahweh and His commands, the obvious answer is that he had learned about them the same way everyone else in the Babylonian and Persian Empires had learned about them—through the witness of Daniel and his friends and through the miraculous interventions that Yahweh had made.

Thus, the deliverance of God's people from the Babylonian exile was similar to the earlier deliverance of God's people from slavery in Egypt—it was accomplished with signs and wonders, miracles. It was clearly an act of God. Both deliverances were also in accordance with prophecy (2 Chronicles 36:22, Ezra 1:1, Genesis 15:12-14, Exodus 3:7-10), God telling in advance what He was going to do. And just as the Israelites had been given wealth by the Egyptians, so the Jews were now given gifts by the Babylonian people (Ezra 1:4, Exodus 3:21-22, 12:35-36)—in both cases, they "plundered" the people who had enslaved them. Finally, both deliverances were in response to the prayers and repentance of God's people (Exodus 3:7, Daniel 9).

The Point of It All

The story of Daniel in the lions' den is known to every child who has been to Sunday school. It is a very dramatic and exciting story. Yet, in reading and teaching the story, we have a tendency to focus on Daniel's remarkable delivery from the lions' den, just as we focus on the dramatic delivery of Hananiah, Mishael and Azariah in chapter 3. We pay no attention to why Daniel was in the lions' den in the first place.

He was thrown into the lion's den because of his dedication to prayer. There are several things we can notice.

1. Regular

The first thing is that Daniel's praying was regular. When he learned about the king's decree, he went home and prayed. It is important to understand that Daniel did not start praying as a result of the king's decree. This was not a political act, an act of protest or defiance. Nor did Daniel stop praying because of the king's decree. He could have said that God wouldn't mind if he temporarily suspended his prayer life due to the unusual circumstances. It would only be for thirty days. Or Daniel could have prayed secretly, without kneeling, so no one would know. Daniel did none of these things. For Daniel's practice of prayer, the king's decree was irrelevant. Daniel followed God's orders, not those of some king whom God could easily replace. The whole point of the administrators' plot is that they knew Daniel could be counted on to pray.

Nor was Daniel's prayer life a virtue of old age, a practice developed as he had the leisure associated with retirement and was facing the prospect of his coming death from old age. We know that when they were still young men, Daniel and his friends responded to the crises in their lives with prayer (Daniel 2:17-18). Prayer was a lifetime habit for him.

One of the other things that is striking is that Daniel prayed three times a day. Sometimes we think we are too busy to pray. Daniel was administering an empire, and he still found time to have three significant prayer sessions every day. Moreover, in the first year of Darius's reign and the third year of Daniel's service under Cyrus, times when he was facing new administrative challenges, Daniel devoted significant extra time to fasting and prayer (Daniel 9:1-3, 10:1-3), prayer for God's Kingdom that had nothing to do with his administrative duties.

And Daniel did not give up. He prayed for seventy years that God would restore His people, Israel.

2. Humble

Daniel 6:10 says that Daniel got down on his knees. All of the kings in this book, Nebuchadnezzar, Belshazzar and Darius, became infatuated with their own power. They became arrogant and failed to recognize that the all-powerful God held their lives in His hand (Daniel 5:23). Daniel, administrator of an empire, knelt in the presence of God. He pleaded for mercy (Daniel 2:18, 9:3). He recognized that God would answer his prayers, not because he deserved it, but only because God was gracious (Daniel 9:18).

3. Thankful

The third remarkable thing about Daniel's prayer here is its content. He asked God for help (Daniel 6:11). This is understandable considering the circumstances, but the verse does not specify what Daniel wanted help with. He might have been asking for deliverance from the threat of the lions' den, but he might also have been asking for help with his administrative duties or help to remain faithful to God. Perhaps it was a general prayer for help with all aspects of his life.

But before he asked for help, Daniel gave thanks to his God (Daniel 6:10). We might wonder what Daniel had to be thankful about. He had no family, he had spent most of his long life in exile, and now he was the object of a death plot by his political enemies. It is human nature to look at the negatives. By the grace of God, Daniel could look at the positives. Through all his long life, God had been with him. God had protected him, given him a successful career and given him purpose and significance. God loved him, and Daniel knew it. Why would he not be thankful? His circumstances were troubling. His situation was blessed.

4. Focused

While we know Daniel prayed for God's help in his own life, there was also a broader aspect to Daniel's prayers. He prayed that he himself would be faithful to God and help build God's Kingdom. He prayed for forgiveness for his people, Israel. He probably prayed for his friend Nebuchadnezzar. He prayed that the pagan people he lived among would learn to know the true God. He prayed that God's glory would fill the earth. In short, in his prayer life, Daniel was focused on God's purposes, not his own.

Bringing It Home

We have a fascination with the miraculous and the experiential in our day. We would love to experience being delivered from our problems as Daniel was delivered from the den of lions and as Hananiah, Mishael and Azariah were delivered from the fiery furnace. We would be thrilled to have the prophetic visions that Daniel had. We would love to see our pagan friends come to faith in Jesus. We long to see our pagan nation come to its senses, practice righteousness and declare that the God of the Bible "is the living God and he endures forever" (Daniel 6:26).

We want all that, but we refuse to pray as Daniel prayed. We are often so preoccupied with handling our urgent problems that we never think to stop and ask God for help. We are too busy to pray three times a day. It is too much trouble for us to fast and pray for our nation for three weeks. We want to have Daniel's blessings without imitating Daniel's life of devotion. We want to know God but rarely spend time in His presence.

Daniel's prayer life stands as a challenge to my own inadequate prayer life. May it also be a challenge to yours. In a pagan society, this is the sixth commitment we need to make:

I will pray diligently, thankfully and expectantly.

Chapter 9
Where Can We Go to Learn about God?
Daniel 9:1-23

The Context

The events of Daniel 9 took place in the first year of the rule of Darius the Mede in Babylon. This was just as Darius was reorganizing the kingdom, Daniel was being thrown into the lions' den for praying "toward Jerusalem" (Daniel 6:10), and the new Persian Empire was consolidating its power. It was also trying to determine what it would do with the people now under its jurisdiction, including the Jews, the remnant of God's people. It was now about 539 BC, and Daniel himself had been in exile for about sixty-six years, since 605 BC. This means that the seventy-year exile foretold by Jeremiah was nearing its end. The Jews would soon be going home, although Daniel himself would almost certainly die in exile.

One of the commentaries I consulted in writing this book devotes 11 lines to Daniel's prayer (Daniel 9:1-19), and over two pages (25 times as much space) to Gabriel's message (Daniel 9:24-27). As I mentioned before, we tend to read the book of Daniel for the prophecies, to try to discover future world events, when the thrust of the book is elsewhere, in teaching us how we can live for God in the midst of world events. The commentary's lack of emphasis on Daniel's prayer is unfortunate because there is a great deal we can learn from Daniel's prayer. We have already looked at Daniel's prayer life in the last chapter, but there are other things we can learn here.

Understanding from the Scriptures

One of the most important aspects of Daniel's prayer is his stated motivation for prayer. He said, "I, Daniel, understood from the Scriptures, according to the word of the LORD given to Jeremiah the prophet..." (Daniel 9:2). It was Daniel's understanding of the Word of God, written in the Bible, that led him to pray.

Where had Daniel learned the Bible, or at least those parts that had been written by that point? We can't be sure. We know that when he first went into exile, he already knew the dietary laws in the books of Moses (Genesis-Deuteronomy) and was determined to keep them (Daniel 1:8). He must have been taught well in Palestine before his exile. It is generally assumed that the Jewish synagogue system, where Jews gathered in local groups (like local Christian churches) to study God's Word, developed during the Babylonian exile. However, this must have taken some time to develop, and there is no record of Daniel ever going to a synagogue. As a high government official, he was probably kept isolated from the bulk of the Jewish exile community to some extent (although he had enough connections to pass on his writings to other Jews, to the point where they could become part of the Bible). When he first went into exile, he seems to have lived in a dormitory with the other exiles being trained for civil service (Daniel 1:3-16). Later on, in Daniel 6, he seems to have had his own house or at least an apartment (6:10). As a high official, he would have had some wealth. Most Jews could not afford a copy of the Scriptures since books (scrolls) had to be copied by hand on expensive parchment (hence the need for Jews to go to the synagogue every week to study the Word of God together). When an Israelite king ascended the throne, he was supposed to write out his own copy of the law by hand. This would be an excellent way of learning the law. As well, the king was supposed to keep the copy with him and read it every day so that he would base his rule on God's laws (Deuteronomy 17:18-20). Daniel was well educated, so perhaps he acquired his own copy as soon as possible. After all, he also had become a top administrator in the Babylonian Empire.

In any case, what comes through very clearly is that Daniel knew the Bible very well. We have already pointed out that Daniel knew the dietary laws (Daniel 1). In Daniel 3, Daniel's three friends showed a knowledge of the Ten Commandments, particularly the commands that they were not to bow before an idol or worship any god but Yahweh (Exodus 20:1-6).

Daniel showed an even more detailed understanding of the Bible here in his prayer in chapter 9. He knew that Yahweh had rescued Israel from a previous exile, in Egypt (Daniel 9:15), and that He had established the Israelites in Palestine to be His people. He knew that Yahweh had chosen Jerusalem to be the place where people would come to learn about Him and worship Him (Daniel 9:16-19; 1 Kings 8, 11:13,32, 14:21; 2 Kings 21:7; 2 Chronicles 6-7, 12:13, 33:7).

More than all this, Daniel understood what God was doing. He understood that God had not chosen Israel and Jerusalem for their own sake but as a base from which to spread the knowledge of God to all people on earth (Daniel 9:15,18-19; Genesis 12:1-3). Therefore, in one sense, it did not matter what happened to Israel and Jerusalem. They were just servants of God's purposes.

But Daniel also understood what God was doing with Israel. He knew that God had given Israel the law or covenant through Moses. The law itself was quite detailed, taking up much of the books of Exodus, Leviticus, Numbers and Deuteronomy. Daniel knew that that law contained detailed promises of blessing if Israel obeyed it, but also detailed curses if Israel disobeyed (Leviticus 26, Deuteronomy 4,28-31). The curses would begin with poor crops and disease and, if Israel did not repent, would culminate in the destruction of

Israel's cities and the exile of its people: "I will turn your cities into ruins...I will scatter you among the nations" (Leviticus 26:30-33). Daniel also knew the history of Israel recorded in the historical books of the Bible (such as Samuel, Kings and Chronicles), that Israel had indeed deserted the true God and suffered the punishments, culminating in exile.

Daniel had also read the prophets (those who had prophesied before the exile) and knew that Yahweh had repeatedly called His people to return to Him. These prophets had not been presenting a new message, just reminding the people of the law of Moses, warning them about the curses and calling for repentance.

The law of Moses not only threatened exile. It also promised that if the Israelites repented in exile, God would restore them to their land: "But if they will confess their sins and the sins of their ancestors...I will remember my covenant" (Leviticus 26:40-45, Deuteronomy 30:1-5). The law specifically stated that the Promised Land would be deserted so that it could have its sabbath rests. The law required the Israelites to let their land lie fallow, grow no crops, for one year in every seven years (Leviticus 25:1-7). It was a good conservation measure, and it was also a good faith-building measure—in those sabbath years, the Israelites would have to rely on God to provide for their needs. Apparently, the Israelites had not observed these sabbath years for the 490 years or so they had been in the Promised Land, so God forced the Israelites out into exile so the land could have the missing seventy sabbath years (2 Chronicles 36:21). Knowing all this, the prophet Jeremiah had written to Daniel and the other exiles that their exile would last seventy years (Jeremiah 29:10). Daniel knew this prophecy (Daniel 9:2). It was now close to seventy years (from 605 BC when Daniel had gone into exile to 539 BC when the Persians conquered Babylon).

Further to all of this, the law required that every fifty years, after every seven sabbath years, there would be a sort of "super sabbath," the Year of Jubilee, when all Israelite slaves would be freed and every Israelite would be restored to his share of the Promised Land—if he had lost his land to debt, for instance (Leviticus 25:8-13). It was a year of restoration and blessing, a year of starting over. It had now been almost 49 years from the time when the last Israelites had gone into exile in 587 BC to the Persian victory in 539 BC. It was time for the Year of Jubilee, the time when every Israelite would be restored to his land.

Daniel knew all of this because he had studied the Bible. He knew what God was doing and why. And he knew what he should do, how he should participate in the plan of God. For the return from exile was not automatic. God had promised return only if the Israelites would repent and "confess their sins and the sins of their ancestors" (Leviticus 26:40). This is what Daniel was doing in his prayer in Daniel 9, confessing his sins and the sins of his people. Daniel knew how to act because he had studied the Bible and knew what God was doing in the world.

Answered Prayer

God sent a messenger, an angel named Gabriel, to answer Daniel's prayer. This was highly unusual, a great privilege. Daniel was indeed "highly esteemed" (Daniel 9:23). The answer, however, was not entirely clear, mixing together several elements.

Daniel was praying for the restoration of Israel to Palestine, so we might expect that God's answer would deal with that. The answer did indicate that there would be a command "to restore and rebuild Jerusalem" and that it would "be rebuilt with streets and a trench" (Daniel 9:25). Yet these details were almost incidental to the answer. The answer did not focus on the rebuilding so much as on the purpose for a rebuilt Jerusalem.

Daniel also prayed a prayer of repentance and a request for forgiveness. It was a passionate plea for help from one who knew that only God could provide help and that God's answer depended on God's mercy, not his own righteousness: "Lord, forgive!" (Daniel 9:19) God's answer, as it often does, went far beyond what was asked, far beyond what Daniel could even imagine (Ephesians 3:20). The answer was not just that God would forgive the Jews and allow them to return to Palestine. It was a promise "to finish transgression, to put an end to sin, to atone for wickedness, to bring in everlasting righteousness, to seal up vision and prophecy and to anoint the Most Holy Place" (Daniel 9:24). Daniel had asked for forgiveness, but this was a promise far beyond the immediate. It was possible that the Jews would return to Palestine, sin and be exiled again—as indeed did happen. But what God was promising was a permanent solution to the sin question, one that would be "everlasting." In short, what God was promising was that He would send His Son Jesus to die on the cross for the sin of all people, not just the Jews. It was a sacrifice far greater than any to be offered in the restored temple; it would be a once-for-all act that would pay for all the sin of all people in all times (Hebrews 7:27, 9:12,25-28; 1 Peter 3:18). It would bring salvation not only to the Jewish remnant but also to the Babylonian wise men and the Persian kings, the poor people in their empire and the people living at the ends of the earth. Those who accepted this forgiveness would not be granted Palestine, but a far better Promised Land, heaven, where there would be no more sin and suffering, death or separation. It was the reason the Jews were being sent back to the Promised Land, to prepare a place for the Messiah, the Savior, to come and die.

Further, God was promising to "seal up vision and prophecy," to complete His revelation in the Bible. Jesus Christ is the ultimate revelation of God (Hebrews 1:1-3), the one who did not come to abolish the law and prophets but to fulfill them (Matthew 5:17). The coming of Jesus completed God's revelation to people. There is no point in waiting for another Messiah, a Mohammed or a Buddha. God said all He was going to say in Jesus.

The promise was also to "anoint the Most Holy Place" (Daniel 9:23). This is a difficult phrase. The word "place" does not appear in the original text, so it is unclear whether the phrase is referring to "the most holy place" or "the most holy one" (that is, a person). In the Old Testament, three kinds of people were anointed with oil, a symbol of the giving of God's Spirit for doing the work of God—prophets, priests and kings. Jesus was all three, so the verse may simply be saying that the "Anointed One" is coming, which is "the Messiah" in Hebrew and "the Christ" in Greek. However, since there is no actual noun in the phrase, it is also possible that it is the most holy "place" that is to be anointed. This might be a reference to the "holy of holies," the innermost room of the temple in Jerusalem where God was said to live and where no one could go except the high priest once a year on the Day of Atonement (Leviticus 16). The New Testament book of Hebrews explains that, as the ultimate high priest, Jesus Christ entered the most holy place, the presence of God, and sacrificed Himself there for the sins of humanity (Hebrews 9). This opened the presence of God to all people redeemed by Christ's sacrifice (Matthew 27:51, Mark 15:38, Luke 23:45). After that, the temple in Jerusalem was no longer needed and was soon destroyed, because after that God would live in His redeemed people, the church of Jesus. So, perhaps the phrase "to anoint the Most Holy" refers to the anointing of the followers of Jesus with the Holy Spirit, the beginning of the great rock which grew into a mountain, the church, the Kingdom of God, which will replace all other kingdoms and fill the earth (Daniel 2:34-35,44-45).

We might get sidetracked by the detail that this would take place in "seventy sevens." The seventy are broken up into three periods: seven, sixty-two and one. The first seven might refer to the time during which the temple and Jerusalem were rebuilt, but it took about twenty years to rebuild the temple and then another eighty years for the walls of Jerusalem to be rebuilt, so perhaps that seven is symbolic, since seven is the number of completion. The next sixty-two sevens, 434 years, are pretty close to the time gap between the completion of the rebuilding of Jerusalem and the birth of Jesus, the Anointed One (Daniel 9:25), the Messiah.

In the last verses, the prophecy gets a little confusing. Two things are happening, two characters are acting—"the Anointed One" and "the ruler"—and it is not always clear which is doing what. Verse 26 says that "the Anointed One will be put to death," a clear reference to the crucifixion of Jesus. "The ruler" will then destroy Jerusalem and its temple again, a pretty clear reference to the Roman destruction of Jerusalem in 70 AD. The setting up of an abomination in the temple (Daniel 9:27) could then refer to the Roman eagles (symbols of the Roman Empire) entering the temple with the conquering army. Jesus referred to this in Matthew 24:15ff, and evidently many early Christians followed Jesus' instruction, fled Jerusalem and avoided being killed in the destruction of the city. The more difficult interpretation concerns the first part of verse 27. One of these two "will confirm a covenant with many for one 'seven'" and "will put an end to sacrifice and offering" in the middle of the seven. If we understand that "the ruler" does this, then it refers to the destruction of the temple by the Romans, although there is no sense in which the Romans confirmed a covenant. Some commentators suggest that "the ruler" also refers to an end-times Antichrist who will make some kind of covenant. That may be. However, the more likely interpretation is that it is "the Anointed One," Jesus, who puts an end to sacrifice (by offering the perfect sacrifice so that no more offerings are needed). He did this in the midst of a seven, after three-and-a-half years of earthly ministry. (It is also possible that this final "week" could refer to the church age, which lasts from the beginning of Jesus' ministry till the end of the world.) It would then also be Jesus who will "confirm a covenant," (a more literal translation might be "cause the covenant to prevail"). This could be a reference to the new covenant God made with people in Jesus, offering to make them part of His eternal Kingdom.

There is one more thing that must be said about the sevens. While we often try to fit them into a historical time scheme, the Bible often uses numbers for symbolic purposes. Seven is the number of completion, since God completed His creation and rested on the seventh day. God here was promising to complete the restoration of His creation and establish the final rest of heaven. But there is also another application. As mentioned above, seven sevens led to the Year of Jubilee, when all debts were cancelled and prisoners were set free. It was the year of forgiveness. Peter asked Jesus: How many times do I have to forgive my brother? He suggested seven times, thinking this was as generous as could be expected. Jesus replied seventy times seven (or possibly seventy-seven times), demonstrating the infinite and expansive forgiveness of God (Matthew 18:21-22, Luke 17:4). Here in Daniel, God was promising to complete forgiveness in "seventy sevens." The number is symbolic of God's infinite forgiveness.

Bringing It Home

I have said that Daniel knew the Bible and therefore what God was doing and how he should cooperate with the plan of God. He knew how to act. The question for us is whether we know the Bible, whether we have used the Bible to get to know God and whether we know how to act.

I knew a man some years ago who had devised a lengthy test of basic biblical knowledge, nothing that called for interpretation, just simple facts. Who followed Moses as leader of Israel? Who was David's father? How many tribes of Israel were there? How many books are in the Old Testament? My friend administered the test to students entering studies at a Christian postsecondary school, beginning about 1950 and continuing for a couple of decades. This was the era when television came in and society was changing rapidly. What my friend discovered was a dramatic decline in basic knowledge of the Bible over a couple of decades.

We are still living in that period of decline today. In fact, if the test were administered today, I expect that the results would be even lower. I grew up in an era when churches held two Sunday services, with preaching both times. There was also adult Sunday school and a mid-week prayer service. Bible teaching was a central part of every one of those services. That meant that every church member had four opportunities for formal study of the Bible every week. Many young people in those days, even those not planning to enter formal ministry, spent a year in Bible school before going on to whatever career they had chosen. Many Christians also read the Bible at home every day, sometimes individually, sometimes as a family, sometimes both.

Today, the average church has one service, and pastors feel enormous pressure to keep the sermon simple, entertaining and popular. Adult Sunday school, if it exists, usually focuses on issues or social studies (parenting, abortion, housing for the poor). Care groups have replaced the mid-week prayer meeting (a positive development in some ways), but there the focus is on "sharing" more than Bible study. Quite a few years ago, my wife and I moved and joined a care group in our new church. The care group explained that we would be studying a Christian book because they had tried studying the Bible the previous year and found it too hard. According to surveys, the majority of Christians rarely read their Bibles other than on Sundays. We are far too busy watching television, listening to music and surfing the Internet, leaving little time for reading the Bible. The Bible is often considered an outmoded form of communication.

Christians today are immersed in the surrounding pagan culture, to the point that they often think and act like pagans. We are not going to become godly with a five-minute devotional after six hours of television. We will become whatever we fill our hearts and minds with.

There are very notable exceptions. However, the reality is that the North American Christian church has become largely biblically illiterate. We don't know who God is, we don't know what He is doing in the world, and we don't know how He wants us to act. As a result, our moral standards have become lax and confused. We don't know what is wrong anymore. We have also become susceptible to every false doctrine that comes along based on psychology, sociology, dreams and the muddled ideas of well-spoken con men. We simply don't know any better.

My father worked long hours. He got up every morning at 5:00 or 5:30 and left for work an hour later. My mother got up to make him a big breakfast. She then had half an hour or an hour before she had to wake the children for school. She would spend that time at the breakfast table with a cup of coffee and the Bible open before her. She said she was "preparing her Sunday school lesson" (she taught children's Sunday school for many years before beginning to teach adult Sunday school after reaching retirement age). What she was really doing was studying the Bible. Those early morning study sessions profoundly changed her life. She became a very godly woman. She would go to church, listen to the sermon and often be disappointed that it felt like "being in kindergarten." Many times, she would see or hear something and know instinctively that "That's not right." She was so immersed in the Bible that she thought and lived biblically, the way God wants people to think and act.

In our increasingly pagan world, this is the seventh commitment we need to make:

I will learn to know God by studying the Bible.

Chapter 10
Doing Exploits
Daniel 7-12

First Vision (Daniel 7)

This book has deliberately focused on the early chapters of Daniel, not on the prophecies in the second half of the book which most modern commentators focus on. This is partly because of my conviction that the early chapters of the book lay the basis for the prophecies in the second half. It is the first half that tells us about Daniel and his situation. In fact, we know more about Daniel as a person than we do about most of the other biblical prophets.

Daniel went into exile in 605 BC. In the ensuing years, he gained a reputation as someone who could interpret dreams, particularly the dreams of Nebuchadnezzar. But there is no record of Daniel receiving any dreams himself until chapter 7. This occurred "in the first year of Belshazzar" (Daniel 7:1). Belshazzar co-ruled Babylon with his absent father, whose reign began in 556 BC, although we don't know for sure that Belshazzar was co-ruler for all of his father's reign. So, we don't know for sure when this vision came, but the earliest it could have come was 556 BC, after Daniel had been in Babylon for almost fifty years. Like the rest of us, Daniel probably expected that he would pass his whole life without ever seeing a prophetic vision.

Daniel's first vision came quite unexpectedly, while he was asleep, dreaming. But the dream was so vivid that when he woke up, he wrote it down, recognizing that it was a message from the one true God.

The dream concerned four beasts that would arise out of the sea (which represents the disorganized mass of humanity). These are four great empires, the same four great empires described in Nebuchadnezzar's dream in Daniel 2: Babylon, Persia, Greece and Rome. Note that:
• The first beast is like a lion, and, as already mentioned, lions were symbols of Babylon.
• The lion was changed into a man, possibly symbolizing Nebuchadnezzar's conversion to worship of the true God.
• The second beast had one side higher than the other, symbolizing that Persia was the dominant partner in the empire of the Medes and Persians.
• The third beast was a panther, which might symbolize the rapid expansion of the empire of Alexander the Greek.
• The third beast had four heads, possibly symbolizing that the Greek Empire was quickly divided into four parts after Alexander's death.
• The fourth beast was partly made of iron like the fourth empire of Daniel 2, and it had ten horns just as the fourth empire in Daniel 2 had ten toes.

There would not be much point in the revelation to this point, since it provided little new information. The Daniel 2 vision concluded with a great rock that destroyed the other kingdoms and grew into a mountain; this was a prophecy of the coming Kingdom of God. This new vision provided more detail about the Kingdom of God. That was the purpose of the new vision, and that is where we should focus our attention.

This new vision presented a vision of the Ancient of Days (the eternal God) on His throne, surrounded by multitudes of worshiping servants, with the fire of judgment flowing from Him. Then "one like a son of man" was given eternal authority over all people on earth (7:13-14). This vision of the coming Kingdom of God focused on Jesus, who came to earth as a man, called himself "the Son of Man" and yet was God, worthy to be worshiped. In his trial before the high priest, Jesus said, "You will see the Son of Man sitting at the right hand of the Mighty One and coming on the clouds of heaven" (Matthew 26:64). In answering the high priest's question as to whether He was the Son of God and the Messiah, Jesus cited this prophecy. He was answering yes, and it was why the Jewish leaders decided to execute Him. It is not entirely clear what the clouds represent—possibly the divinity of Jesus (since God appeared as a cloud in the Old Testament and was said to ride on the clouds: Deuteronomy 33:26), possibly blessing (since clouds bring rain), possibly judgment (since clouds bring fury and lightning) or possibly the resurrected followers of Jesus (Hebrews 12:1). In any case, this image became the symbol of the returning Jesus in the New Testament (see Matthew 24:30, 1 Thessalonians 4:17, Revelation 1:7).

Daniel's vision in chapter 7 was quite a detailed prophecy, describing both the coming of Jesus and the coming Kingdom of God. This Kingdom would be given to "the holy people of the Most High" (Daniel 7:18,27: true believers of all nations and not just the believing Jews), but this would be a spiritual Kingdom, not like the other kingdoms and certainly not like the flawed "Christian kingdom" that Constantine and many other "Christian" rulers have attempted to set up.

Then Daniel demonstrated a fault that many of the rest of us share. Having been shown the glory of the Kingdom of God, he became distracted by wanting to know more about the last of the human kingdoms. He did not ask God or His Son Jesus, but "one of those standing there" (Daniel 7:16), one of the servants of God, perhaps an angel. The answer he received was detailed but not clear. It concerned a king who would oppress "the holy people" (Daniel 7:21). It is not certain who this is. It could be Julius Caesar, who replaced a trio of Roman leaders to become the first (unofficial) emperor and changed the calendar (July is named after him). It could be Vespasian, who was about the 11th Roman emperor (depending on whether we count emperors whose reigns were brief and disputed) and who destroyed Jerusalem with his son Titus in 70 AD. It could be a reference to all the Roman emperors. It could also be a reference to an end-times Antichrist. It doesn't greatly matter. What matters is that "his power will be taken away and completely destroyed forever" and that all kingdoms will be handed over to "the holy people of the Most High" (Daniel 7:26-27).

This boastful king would attack the saints for "a time, times and half a time" (Daniel 7:25). This seems to pick up the recurring half a week idea. Again, it is difficult to determine what is meant. It could refer to the three-and-a-half-year Roman invasion of Palestine that culminated in the destruction of Jerusalem in 70 AD. It could refer to the three-and-a-half-century Roman persecution of Christianity until the empire was "Christianized." It could refer to both and to other periods as well. It could also be symbolic. There is probably some symbolism in the way the number is phrased. The Hebrew does not say "three and a half," but the more awkward "time, times and half a time." There is a mathematical progression. There is first one time and then a doubling to two times. One might expect there would be a further doubling to four times. One plus two plus four would be seven, the number of completeness, which is what those who oppose God often claim they are achieving. But they can never achieve it, and their reign is cut short. Only God can achieve completeness.

Second Vision (Daniel 8)

The second vision also came as a dream while Daniel was sleeping. In the dream, Daniel saw himself beside the Ulai Canal in the city of Susa in the province of Elam. This was still likely part of the Babylonian Empire, but it was the part where the Persians lived, so we might expect that the prophecy would concern the kingdom of the Medes and Persians, who would soon conquer Babylon. The prophecy starts with Persia but soon moves on to the next great empire, Greece. In particular, it deals with one of the four kingdoms that would arise out of the Greek Empire and one of its kings, Antiochus IV. Antiochus claimed to be a god. In 169 BC, he entered the innermost part of Yahweh's temple in Jerusalem and replaced the worship of Yahweh with worship of the Greek gods. This caused the Jewish people to rebel. They drove out Antiochus's forces, they re-consecrated the temple, and for a time Judah was an independent state once again. Although they are both called "horns" (a symbol of power), Antiochus should not be confused with the horn of the previous prophecy, who was part of the Roman Empire, not the Greek.

What was the point of this prophecy, and why was it given to Daniel? It does not concern the setting up of the Kingdom of God under Jesus, so why did God bother to give the vision? The most logical answer is that God gave this vision so that the Jewish people would know that these events were going to happen and so that the Jewish people would not be confused about their significance. When Judas Maccabaeus led the revolt, re-consecrated the temple and re-established Judah as an independent kingdom, there was a danger that the Jewish people might think that this was the Kingdom of God promised in Daniel's prophecies and that Judas Maccabaeus was the Messiah. It wasn't, and he wasn't. God's promised Kingdom was much greater than anything that Judas Maccabaeus could achieve, and God didn't want His people to be confused.

The more significant part of this vision was the appearance of "one who looked like a man." A man then spoke from the canal, telling the angel Gabriel to explain the vision to Daniel (Daniel 8:15-16). As in the previous vision, the words of explanation were provided by one of God's messengers (Daniel 7:15), now named Gabriel. Gabriel was also the messenger who told of the imminent arrival of Jesus in the New Testament (Luke 1:19,26). It is not absolutely clear here who the "one who looked like a man" is. The name "Gabriel" comes from two words: *geber*, which means "valiant one" or warrior," and *el*, which literally means "mighty" but which is the word commonly used for God. So, the "one who looked like a man" could refer to Gabriel. Or the "one who looked like a man" could refer to the man who spoke from the middle of the river, the "one like a son of man" from the previous chapter (Daniel 7:13); that is, he could be Jesus, who ordered the angel to explain the prophecy to Daniel. Gabriel and the Son of Man also appear in Daniel's next visions.

Third Vision (Daniel 9)

We have already looked at the third vision. This vision came in the first year of Darius, after Daniel had spent an extended period in prayer and fasting. Daniel was not praying for a vision but was praying a prayer of repentance on behalf of his people and asking God to restore the Jews to their land.

This prayer displays a remarkable summary of the character of Yahweh. Daniel said that God was "great and awesome" (Daniel 9:4). Unlike the Babylonians, who thought of their gods as limited, Daniel knew that Yahweh was the all-powerful God who had created everything in the universe, who knew everything and who could do anything. Also, Daniel knew that God was "righteous in everything he does" (Daniel 9:7,14,16), that He had imposed righteous laws on human beings (Daniel 9:5) and that He enforced those laws by punishing those who broke them (Daniel 9:7,11-16). As well, Daniel knew that God was loving (Daniel 9:4), merciful and forgiving (Daniel 9:9,18). Daniel knew that God had rescued the people of Israel from Egypt (Daniel 9:15) and made a covenant with Israel and that in His mercy He had sent prophets to remind Israel of that covenant and call Israel to repent. Daniel knew that God had acted to create "a Name" for Himself (Daniel 9:15,18,19), to reveal Himself to all of humanity. Because Daniel knew the character of God, he could pray, basing his prayer on God's righteous and loving nature. Because Daniel knew that God's purpose was to spread the knowledge of God to all humanity, he could act in cooperation with God's plan. And God responded to that prayer by providing a vision outlining more of God's plan.

There seems to be an increasing intimacy to these visions. This one occurred while Daniel was awake "about the time of the evening sacrifice" (Daniel 9:21). Daniel immediately recognized the messenger as Gabriel.

This vision described the Jews' return from exile, Jesus' provision of forgiveness for sins and a further destruction of Jerusalem. The vision reflects what Daniel already knew about Yahweh's nature as righteous and loving—God would act in the future as He had in the past. God would complete His plan of redemption for humanity.

Fourth Vision (Daniel 10-12)

The fourth vision occurred a little later, in the third year of Cyrus, and it occurred in broad daylight and in public, although it also came after Daniel had spent a considerable time in prayer and fasting (Daniel 10:2-3). We are not told why Daniel was mourning. It may have been over the general sinfulness and suffering in the world. Or perhaps it was because Daniel saw his countrymen heading home and he realized that he never would, that he would die in exile. Daniel was with some other men by the Tigris River, which is the eastern of the two great rivers in Babylon, while many of his fellow Jews had probably gathered by the Euphrates to get ready to go home.

This took place outside the city since only Daniel and his companions seem to have been in the vicinity. His companions did not see the vision itself, but only enough to drive them away in fear. This was similar to the experience of the apostle Paul on the road to Damascus in the New Testament, in which he saw and heard Jesus while his companions saw only light and heard a noise (Acts 9:1-8). Here also Daniel saw Jesus, although that name is not used. What Daniel saw was a shining man. Perhaps he recognized this man as the same person as the "one like a son of man" who had "authority, glory and sovereign power" in his first vision (Daniel 7:13-14). It was a vision of Jesus the God man. This shining man vision (Daniel 10:4-6) is the same as the one John saw in Revelation (Revelation 1:12-16), although the Revelation passage has some additional details. The reaction to an encounter with the great God, when people see Jesus as He really is, is to fall awestruck on the ground before Him. This is what Daniel did (Daniel 10:8,15-17). This was the reaction of Paul (Acts 9:4-9) and of Isaiah (Isaiah 6:5) and of Ezekiel (Ezekiel 1:28) and of John (Revelation 1:17) and of many other biblical characters who encountered God. Job said, "My ears had heard of you but now my eyes have seen you. Therefore I despise myself and repent in dust and ashes" (Job 42:5-6). When we really encounter the true God, it changes our perspective and our life.

In Daniel 11, the shining man related in detail a series of wars which would take place between two of the four kingdoms into which Alexander's Greek Empire would be divided. The King of the North was the Seleucid dynasty, which ruled in Syria, and the King of the South was the Ptolemaic dynasty, which ruled in Egypt. Note that while these kingdoms considered themselves the center of the world, God's focus was on the tiny remnant of Judah in Palestine between them. From this perspective, the Seleucids were north and the Ptolemys south. The details can be matched to specific events in history, but in the end they seem not very important. This chapter details a dreary and confusing repetition of war, intrigue, arrogance and betrayal. It is perhaps a summary of the history of humanity, as generations of the unscrupulous expend their lives struggling for supremacy, riches and power, but in the end it all proves temporary and unsatisfying, "a chasing after the wind" (Ecclesiastes 1:14).

Because the series of wars were fought between the Seleucids to the north and the Ptolemys to the south, the Jews between them were subject to repeated invasions. Of particular note is Antiochus IV, who was also described in

Daniel's second vision and who set up pagan worship in the rebuilt temple of Yahweh in Jerusalem. Antiochus, who is now a little known figure in history, called himself Antiochus Epiphanes (Manifest) because he claimed to be a human "manifestation" or appearance of the divine. In other words, he claimed to be what Jesus really was, God in human form. Some scholars see the Daniel 11 description of Antiochus in the second century BC as also describing an end-times Antichrist. This is certainly possible, but as the apostle John said, there are many antichrists (1 John 2:18). Throughout history, from Adam and Eve in the Garden of Eden (Genesis 3:4-6) to Nebuchadnezzar and Darius, at the instigation of Satan, people have repeatedly been setting themselves up as gods, seeing themselves as the center of the universe. This detailed history in Daniel 11 thus represents the whole sordid sweep of human history—and it is here that it has significance for us. For we believers in the true God are almost always placed in a pagan culture, surrounded by war, intrigue, arrogance and suffering. And it is here that we are called to worship and proclaim the God of Heaven to the pagans around us, just as Daniel did.

Who Is in Control?

In the last couple of centuries, some commentators have suggested that the book of Daniel must have been written in the second century BC rather than in the sixth century BC. This is because the prophecies about the Persian and Greek Empires are so accurate that these scholars are convinced Daniel couldn't possibly have predicted them ahead of time. This is, of course, true. Daniel could not have predicted these things accurately. Even the best political analyst could not have predicted them. But the God of the Bible could. And the God of the Bible did. God is not limited by time. The thing is, these commentators are not really doubting Daniel's ability to predict the future; they are doubting God's ability. What these commentators fail to account for is that Daniel's prophecies also accurately foretold the Roman Empire and the coming of Jesus.

What these prophecies make clear is that the God of the Bible, the God whom Daniel worshiped, knows the future. More than that, these prophecies make clear that the God of the Bible controls the future. This is far from obvious to us. We ask questions such as: Why did God allow the Jews to be conquered by the Babylonians? Why did God allow Hananiah, Mishael and Azariah to be thrown into a furnace or Daniel to be thrown into a den of lions? Why would God allow Antiochus Epiphanes to desecrate His temple? Sometimes we understand the reason (the furnace and the den of lions demonstrated God's power and nature to pagan peoples), but sometimes we do not. But what is clear is that God does control the future and that He has a great plan that He is working out. Remember that Nebuchadnezzar did not conquer Jerusalem; it was not a case of his gods proving to be more powerful than Israel's God. Daniel 1:2 says that "the Lord delivered Jehoiakim king of Judah into his hand, along with some of the articles from the temple of God." Nebuchadnezzar conquered only because God determined that he would conquer. God later deposed Nebuchadnezzar for a time to teach him this lesson (Daniel 4). God then arranged for the Persians to conquer Babylon as a judgment on Babylon (Daniel 5).

And what was the over-riding purpose behind all of this? The point to which God was directing history was the establishment of the Kingdom of God, the great mountain that would replace all human kingdoms (Daniel 2). It was the coming of Jesus "to finish transgression, to put an end to sin, to atone for wickedness, to bring in everlasting righteousness" (Daniel 9:24), to offer salvation to every person on earth. It was to inform all the peoples of the world about God's greatness and about the promise of the coming Kingdom, so that when Jesus came, magicians from the pagan east would travel many miles to worship Him and people "from every nation under heaven" (Acts 2:5) would be ready to welcome Him.

The People Who Know Their God

I began this book with the assertion that the people of God in North America are immersed in a pagan culture. This is not an unusual situation in history. The same situation existed in Daniel's day and in many other periods of human history since. In this sense, the history related in Daniel and prophesied in Daniel can be seen as representative of human history. On the one hand, there are all the pagan kingdoms marked by war and cruelty and arrogance as kings claim divine authority. As Nebuchadnezzar and Belshazzar and Darius did, they set themselves up as gods (Daniel 11:36) and worship power ("a god of fortresses": Daniel 11:38). They blaspheme "the God of gods" (Daniel 11:36), desecrate His temple (Daniel 11:31), attack God's people (Daniel 11:33) and even attempt to corrupt God's people (Daniel 11:32). But all the while, the true God is in control, and He is able to humble and change the most powerful kings (as He did with Nebuchadnezzar) or destroy them (as He did with Belshazzar). Indeed, all who oppose God and His eternal Kingdom will ultimately be destroyed (Daniel 11:45, 12:2).

One of the things that stands out most clearly in the closing chapters of Daniel is the distinction between the wicked and the wise, pagans and the people of God. The wicked will end in "shame and everlasting contempt" while the wise will receive "everlasting life" (Daniel 12:2). The thing that we must remember is to take the long perspective as Daniel did. The pagans might have overrun our Jerusalems, we might suffer in exile for many years, we might be thrown into fire or thrown to the lions, but all of this is temporary. All of the powerful and arrogant empires of the world will be swept away, replaced by the everlasting Kingdom of God.

In light of this, what should be our response? Our response should be that of Daniel, Hananiah, Mishael and Azariah—to live for God in a pagan society. The closing chapters of Daniel call these people "wise." Even though some of God's people will betray God and be corrupted (Daniel 11:30,32), those who are wise will stand fast. They might be killed by the sword, burned, captured and plundered (Daniel 11:33, as Daniel and his fellow Jews were), but they will stand fast nevertheless. They will suffer much "distress," but they "will be delivered" (Daniel 12:1). Some of them might stumble for a time, but they will be forgiven and restored (Daniel 11:35). Rather than worry about their own lives, in the midst of persecution, they will "instruct many" (Daniel 11:33), "shine like the brightness of the heavens" (Daniel 12:3, Philippians 2:14-15) and "lead many to righteousness" (Daniel 12:3). The wise will "be refined, purified and made spotless" (Daniel 11:35, 12:10), while "the wicked will continue to be wicked" (Daniel 12:10). The wise will understand, while the wicked will not (Daniel 12:10). The wise will be given "everlasting life," while the wicked will end in "shame and everlasting contempt" (Daniel 12:2). The book ends with reassurance for Daniel and those like him. God told Daniel to "go your way" (Daniel 12:9,13), to keep his focus on the Kingdom of God rather than on the machinations of pagan empires outlined in the prophecies. In short, he was to keep on doing what he had been doing. The phrase also suggests that it was time for Daniel to pass on, to die. But God told Daniel not to worry about it because at the end of the world he would rise again and receive his "allotted inheritance" (Daniel 12:13). This is an astonishing answer to Daniel's prayer of repentance in Daniel 9. The exile who never got to go home to Israel's Promised Land will receive his portion in a far greater promised land, the everlasting Kingdom of God.

When I have taught the book of Daniel in care groups and adult Sunday school classes, I have sometimes asked if there is a key verse which summarizes the message of this remarkable Bible book. Often people will respond with Daniel 2:28: "There is a God in heaven who reveals mysteries." This is an important message, but it is only part of the message. Instead, I think the key verse in Daniel is in the second half of Daniel 11:32: "the people who know their God will firmly resist him" (NIV). The New International Version is not very accurate here. It tries to apply the verse to its immediate context, but the verse has a broader meaning. Literally, what it says is: "The people who know their God will stand firm and do." The New American Standard Bible says, "The people who know their God will display strength and take action." The King James Version says, "The people that do know their God shall be strong, and do exploits." There are three key things here. First, the distinguishing feature of the wise is that they know the true God. Daniel, Hananiah, Mishael and Azariah could act differently from everyone else around them because they knew the real God, Yahweh, the God of Heaven, the God who revealed Himself to the people of Israel, the God of the Bible. If we want to be different from the pagans, we must first believe differently. Second, these people who know their God will stand firm or be strong. This was what allowed Daniel and his friends to refuse to break God's laws by eating the king's food. It was what allowed Hananiah, Mishael and Azariah to refuse to worship Nebuchadnezzar's golden idol. It was what allowed Daniel to continue to pray when Darius had forbidden it. Third, the people who know their God will be able to take action, do exploits, resist the antichrists who claim to be gods, work for the good of the evil city they live in and lead even many pagans to righteousness, including powerful emperors such as Nebuchadnezzar. They can turn the world upside down. We may be immersed in a pagan culture, but we do not have to become pagans. As Daniel and his friends so amply demonstrated, it is possible to live for God in a pagan society.

Study Guide

This book is designed as a study guide to the book of Daniel. In using it, I suggest you follow these five steps.

1. Pray that the God who inspired the Bible will reveal its meaning to you.

2. Read the Scripture for each chapter. That is, you should begin where we should always begin, with the Word of God. When I have taught this material in small groups, I have often arranged to have the Bible passages read as "readers' theater." That is, one member of the group would read the narrative verses, and other members would read the words of the various characters. In larger groups, the Bible passages could even be presented as a dramatic play by a group of well-prepared actors. Bible stories are wonderfully dramatic, and it is important to sense the interaction between the people in the book and understand the dynamic power of this story of Daniel.

3. Read the relevant chapter of this book.

4. Use the following study questions to stimulate discussion of the Scripture and the specific chapter of the book. Neither the book nor the study questions are presented as authoritative in their own right but only as guides into the authoritative truth of God's Word.

5. Practice what you read and learn. This book is not intended primarily to provide knowledge but to stir readers to obey the teaching of Scripture. "The people who know their God will display strength and take action" (Daniel 11:32, NASB).

Study Questions

Chapter 1
1. To what extent are we living in a pagan, God-defying society? Will our Jerusalem fall?
2. Where am I personally facing pressure from a God-defying society?
3. Does the present or future or at least certain aspects of them appear hopeless? What do I think I can do about whatever difficult situation I am facing? If I knew what to do, am I prepared to take action?

Chapter 2
1. What moral pressures do we face today? On what issues are we tempted to compromise?
2. What moral temptations am I personally facing?
3. Have I ever used the excuse, "Everyone's doing it, so it must be okay"?
4. Do I treat civil authorities with respect?
5. How can I go about seeking civil permission to obey God's laws?
6. What will I do if that permission is denied?
7. Whom do I see as the real enemy? Do I focus on fighting sin, evil and Satan? What is my attitude to people who have beliefs different from mine, or even people who try to pressure me into doing something I believe is wrong?
8. Have I resolved to avoid personal moral defilement?

Chapter 3

1. When I am faced with a crisis, what do I do? Pray? Ask others to pray? Panic? Find out more details? Trust God? Blame someone?
2. What is my understanding of God?
    a. Do I believe that there is only one God?
    b. Do I believe that God is the Creator of the heavens and the earth?
    c. Do I believe that God is all-powerful and knows everything, past, present and future?
    d. Do I believe that God is holy, perfectly moral? Do I believe that God commands me to be holy, perfectly moral?
3. It has been said that we become like the gods we worship. To what extent is that true?
4. If we believe in a God who can do anything and who reserves that authority to Himself (that is, if we believe that God can perform miracles but that whether He does so is entirely up to Him), what does that say about modern Christian ideas such as "praying with authority"?
5. What do I think about other religions? Are they alternate paths to God? Is there some truth in them? Are they false, inspired by Satan? What does God think about them?
6. What do I think about the followers of false religions? Would I go out of my way to save them, or do I think they deserve condemnation?
7. Is my focus on building the Kingdom of God or on building my own kingdom? Do I see what God is doing in history, or am I preoccupied with my own survival?

Chapter 4

1. What are the issues, big and small, where I must choose between following the true God and worshiping false ones?
2. Today, in North America, the state does not threaten to execute us immediately if we do not bow down to an idol or worship a false god. But what false gods are we tempted to worship? Where does the pressure come from?

3. At what point does the state itself become a false god demanding our highest allegiance? What loyalty do I owe to the state, my nation? At what point does loyalty to my nation conflict with loyalty to the one true God?

4. Is my nation more like Judah (the "people of God") or the Babylonian Empire? Even if I consider my nation to be like the people of God, could my loyalty to that nation conflict with my loyalty to God? Did Daniel give undivided loyalty to Judah?

5. Nebuchadnezzar was amazed by his encounter with "the God of Shadrach, Meshach and Abednego" (Daniel 3:28). What do those around you think of the God you portray? How impressive is the God of _____ (insert your name)?

6. Do I believe that God "lives among humans" (Daniel 2:11)? Do I really believe that God wants to have a personal relationship with every human being? Do I have a personal relationship with God? Why or why not? Would it make any difference if I took a public stand, declaring my loyalty to the one true God?

Chapter 5

1. Do I believe that everything I have is a gift of God (1 Corinthians 4:7)? Or do I think that I have earned my money, my position, my success?

2. Have I humbled myself before the God of Heaven, and have I committed myself to building His Kingdom rather than my own? If so, how is that evident in my actions?

3. Daniel seems to have grown to love the pagan king Nebuchadnezzar. Do I love the pagan people around me? Whom in particular do I need to learn to love?

4. Do I have the courage to tell people around me that they need to repent and accept Jesus into their lives? How can I balance this harsh message with love?

5. Daniel managed to tell Nebuchadnezzar that he was a sinner and needed to change without angering Nebuchadnezzar. How did he do this? How can I do this with the "sinners" I encounter? What role do love and humility

play in this? Was Nebuchadnezzar willing to listen to Daniel because he knew Daniel loved him and only told him the bad news because he knew he must? Do I relish telling the bad news? Or do I tell it with tears?

6. Nebuchadnezzar and probably some of his magicians came to worship the Most High God. Do I believe that God can change the minds of the most pagan people around me?

7. How will I tell the pagan people around me about the Most High God? What am I afraid of? What is holding me back?

Chapter 6

1. In what ways could I be a more productive member of my society? Will the world be a better place because of what I say and do? Am I more interested in what I can get out of my job (such as money) than in what I contribute? Would people at my place of work say I am "trustworthy and neither corrupt nor negligent" (Daniel 6:4)?

2. What commitment do I have to raising the next generation of God's people? Do I see my parenting role as a responsibility given to me by God?

3. Do I want my nation to be peaceful, prosperous and blessed? Or do I secretly want God to punish my neighbors for their sinful lifestyles? Do I pray regularly for the welfare of the society around me? Why or why not?

4. Whom do I consider to be my enemies? Do I love them and pray for them and want God to bless them (Matthew 5:43)?

5. What prophecies am I listening to? Do these modern prophecies and interpretations agree with the true God who is moral and loving? Do they lead me to repentance and dependence on God? Or do they lead to arrogance and complacency?

6. What do I believe is going to happen to my nation? Does this belief help or hinder me in fulfilling God's will for my life? Regardless of what God might be planning in the long run, what am I doing to build God's Kingdom here and now?

7. How do we know what God wants of us today living in our society? What do we know, and what has God not told us? Do

we believe that God has plans for our future, plans to prosper and not harm us (Jeremiah 29:11)? To what extent is this promise to the Jews in the sixth century BC applicable to us today?

8. In the past, God punished false prophets. Have I ever been guilty of confusing my wishes with the will of God? What should I do when apparently equally sincere Christians hold views opposite to mine? How can I guard myself against unjustifiably claiming God's approval for my viewpoint?

Chapter 7

1. How many times has God directly intervened in my life? How have I responded? Am I becoming more open to God, or am I slowly hardening in my attitude toward Him?

2. Why do some people respond positively to God and others do not?

3. Do I really believe in the all-powerful God of the Bible, who demands that the people He created live morally? Do I really believe that God judges people on the way they live their lives and the way they respond to Him? Am I constantly aware that God knows everything I think and do and I live under the judgment of God? Would I really sometimes rather have a god of wood or stone that I can control?

4. What is the focus in my life with God? Am I more focused on whether God is serving me well or on whether I am serving God well? In my Bible reading, do I look for God's promises or God's commands? Are my prayers focused on finding God's will so that I can serve Him, or are my prayers long lists of things that I want God to do for me? Am I seeking God's help in building my kingdom, or am I willing to sacrifice myself to build His Kingdom?

5. Consider the apostle Paul's attitude in Acts 20:24 and 2 Timothy 4:6-8. Will I finish well? Have I become bitter or discouraged? Have I become "weary in doing good" (Galatians 6:9)? Am I serving as well as I did earlier in my life? In what areas am I becoming more godly? In what areas and in what ways am I becoming less godly?

Chapter 8

1. Do I know how to pray? Do I really have an intimate relationship with God where we talk as friends? Do I even believe that is possible?
2. Do I pray regularly every day? What excuses do I have for not doing so? Am I "too busy"?
3. Am I embarrassed to pray in public? Even if I won't be thrown into a lions' den, am I afraid of what people might say or think?
4. Are my prayers as broad as Daniel's were? Do I just pray for myself and my needs, or do I pray for issues concerning the Kingdom of God? Do I pray that Christian people today would be released from the bondage of indifference, shallowness and sin? Do I pray that parents will love their children instead of aborting them or abusing them? Do I pray that child abuse, marriage breakups and sexually transmitted diseases will be washed away in a flood of sexual morality? Do I pray that peace and love will replace hate and violence? Do I pray that my nation will practice justice and mercy in its foreign policy? Do I pray that other nations will practice justice and mercy and righteousness? Do I pray that knowledge of the God of the Bible will overwhelm the false religions that billions of people still follow? Do I pray for the establishment and expansion of the Kingdom of God till it fills the whole earth?
5. Daniel prayed and asked for God's mercy on the basis of God's love. He did so while recognizing that he and his people were sinful and did not deserve God's mercy, did not deserve God's blessed response. Are our prayers like that? Are we humble and conscious of our own sin? Are we ever guilty of barging into prayer, flinging out orders and expecting that God has to give us what we want because we deserve it?
6. Do I believe that prayer changes things? Or do I think it is more important to act, to write letters, stage demonstrations, initiate court challenges, be active, do something? Do I believe that my actions will achieve more than God's?

Chapter 9

1. Does Daniel's prayer in Daniel 9:4-19 shed any light on the study question for chapter 4: Is my nation more like Judah (the "people of God") or the Babylonian Empire? Even if I consider my nation to be like the people of God, could my loyalty to the people of God conflict with my loyalty to God? Did Daniel give undivided loyalty to Judah?
2. Could my nation be in need of a sabbath rest? What kinds of prophetic voices is my nation ignoring? What kind of disasters will it take before my nation repents and turns to God?
3. What attention does my church give to the Bible? Has this changed in the last few years? Is further change necessary? How can I be part of the change?
4. How often do I read the Bible on my own? Do I read it, or really study it? If I believed my life depended on it (it does), would I study it more? What would have to change in my life in order for me to study the Bible more?
5. Do I feel confident that I can read and understand the Bible? Do I need help?
6. Do I understand that God sometimes responds to prayers with answers that go far beyond my expectations? Do I fully appreciate the greatness of the salvation that Jesus provided by dying on the cross? Do I understand that He paid for the sins of all people in all times? Do I really understand seventy times seven forgiveness?
7. Do I know all I need to know about God? About what He is doing in this world? About what I should be doing? If someone comes to me for help, can I give biblical answers?
8. Am I so immersed in the biblical worldview that I automatically respond to life in godly ways?

Chapter 10

1. Am I one of the wise or one of the wicked? If I am one of the wise, how can I keep from forsaking or violating my covenant

with God (Daniel 11:28,30)? If I am one of the wicked, do I now want to change my status?

2. What experiences do I have of standing firm and doing exploits?

3. Do I believe it is too late for me to have a significant experience with God? (Daniel was probably in his sixties when he received his first vision.)

4. Consider Daniel's question in Daniel 7:19. Have I ever been more interested in the sordid details of this present world than in the vision of the Kingdom of God?

5. Do I really believe in and trust the God of the Bible even when the forces of paganism seem to be over-running the people of God?

6. Consider the claims of human systems to achieve completeness, such as Marx's claim that there would be an ideal world once communism was established, or psychologists' claims to produce whole personalities, or the anti-Christian claim to produce a perfect world once the hang-ups of religion are abolished. (Remember John Lennon's song "Imagine all the people living lives of peace" once there is "no religion.") How does Daniel's vision of "time, times and half a time" relate to such claims?

7. Have I ever "stumbled"? Do I believe that God can use that experience to refine and purify me? (Daniel 11:35)

8. Have I instructed any or led any to righteousness (Daniel 11:33, 12:3)? Am I "blameless and pure"? Do I shine "like stars in the universe" as I "hold firmly to the word of life" in "a warped and crooked generation" (Philippians 2:12-16)?

9. Is there something I have wanted all my life or for a long time that I now realize I may never receive? Am I content to wait for the "allotted inheritance" (Daniel 12:13) God has for me?

10. Consider Daniel's prayer in Daniel 9. Do I know God as great and awesome, righteous in everything He does, loving, merciful and forgiving? Do I know God well enough to stand firm and do exploits? Am I committed to living for God in a pagan society?

My Commitment

Recognizing that a God-defying society wants to squeeze me into its mold:
- I resolve to avoid personal moral defilement (Daniel 1:8).
- I will worship only the true God, even at the cost of my life (Daniel 3:17-18).
- Knowing that God can convert pagans, I will witness (Daniel 4:37).
- I will seek the peace and prosperity of the society in which I live (Jeremiah 29:4-7).
- I will remain faithful to God's call, serving Him till the end of my life (Daniel 5).
- I will pray diligently, thankfully and expectantly (Daniel 6:10-11).
- I will learn to know God by studying the Bible (Daniel 9:3).
- I will trust God, and I will do my part to let God build His Kingdom through me, knowing that He is in control and that He has revealed what He is doing in the world (Daniel 4:17, 9:24).

"The people who know their God will display strength and take action." (*Daniel 11:32, NASB*)

Signed _____

James R. Coggins is a professional writer and editor based in Abbotsford, British Columbia, Canada. He has BA and MA degrees from McMaster University, a Diploma in Christian Studies from Regent College and a PhD from the University of Waterloo. He has served as an editor of Christian magazines and written a wide variety of materials, including devotional and academic articles. His previous books include *John Smyth's Congregation: English Separatism, Mennonite Influence and the Elect Nation*; *Wonders and the Word: An Examination of Issues Raised by John Wimber and the Vineyard Movement* (co-edited with Paul Hiebert); *Who's Grace?*; *Desolation Highway*; *Mountaintop Drive*; *Springtime in Winnipeg*; and *1995: Je me souviens*. His website is: www.coggins.ca

www.ingramcontent.com/pod-product-compliance
Lightning Source LLC
Chambersburg PA
CBHW070605010526
44118CB00012B/1447